Practicing the Ordinary Supernatural Presence of God

Practicing the Ordinary Supernatural Presence of God

WALKING WITH JESUS AND THE SPIRIT
IN THE ORDINARY SUPERNATURAL

JOHN JEFFERSON DAVIS

CASCADE *Books* · Eugene, Oregon

PRACTICING THE ORDINARY SUPERNATURAL PRESENCE OF GOD
Walking with Jesus and the Spirit in the Ordinary Supernatural

Copyright © 2021 John Jefferson Davis. All rights reserved. Except for brief quotations in critical publications or reviews, no part of this book may be reproduced in any manner without prior written permission from the publisher. Write: Permissions, Wipf and Stock Publishers, 199 W. 8th Ave., Suite 3, Eugene, OR 97401.

Cascade Books
An Imprint of Wipf and Stock Publishers
199 W. 8th Ave., Suite 3
Eugene, OR 97401

www.wipfandstock.com

PAPERBACK ISBN: 978-1-7252-8500-2
HARDCOVER ISBN: 978-1-7252-8501-9
EBOOK ISBN: 978-1-7252-8502-6

Cataloguing-in-Publication data:

Names: Davis, John Jefferson, author.

Title: Practicing the ordinary supernatural presence of God : walking with Jesus and the spirit in the ordinary supernatural / John Jefferson Davis.

Description: Eugene, OR: Cascade Books, 2021 | Includes bibliographical references.

Identifiers: ISBN 978-1-7252-8500-2 (paperback) | ISBN 978-1-7252-8501-9 (hardcover) | ISBN 978-1-7252-8502-6 (ebook)

Subjects: LCSH: Church renewal. | Church and the world. | Attention—Religious aspects—Christianity. | Technology—Religious aspects—Christianity.

Classification: BR517 .D28 2021 (print) | BR517. (ebook)

CONTENTS

PREFACE

THE PURPOSE OF THIS book is to help you rediscover and enjoy the supernatural experience at the heart of the New Testament church's spiritual vitality and remarkable growth: a *conscious awareness of the joyful, life-changing presence of the living God in the midst of his people.* The New Testament's supernatural quality of life is still available today.

The title *Practicing the Ordinary Supernatural Presence of God* highlights two crucial ideas: the *presence of God* and the *ordinary supernatural.* The title recalls Brother Lawrence's devotional classic, *The Practice of the Presence of God*, and offers a richer biblical basis for it. God's presence in the midst of his people and their enjoyment of that presence is a central theme of the Bible from Genesis to Revelation and is at the heart of our salvation and Christian worship. This book shows how to experience and enjoy God's presence in Sunday worship and daily living.

The concept of the *ordinary supernatural* enlarges usual understandings of supernatural. God is supernaturally present not only in extraordinary supernatural acts that are visible and spectacular—miracles, dramatic healings, resurrections of the dead, demons cast out, speaking in tongues—but also in the Holy Spirit's less visible and quieter actions: illuminating Scripture, convicting of sin, converting sinners, growing the Spirit's fruit, forming Christlike character. In the long run, the ordinary supernatural actions of the Spirit are more important for the church's growth than spectacular miracles whose effects may not last. Healings can be temporary, but the fruit of the Spirit lasts into eternity.

vii

As the secular world's power over nature increases, the church must live by power that is more than natural—by the ordinary supernatural power of the Spirit. Living in the ordinary supernatural is possible now, sustainable over a lifetime, and consistent with Scripture and sound doctrine.

This book focuses on three biblical chapters (Acts 2, Matthew 28, John 17); three Christian doctrines (Trinity, union with Christ, Holy Spirit); and three spiritual practices (worship, meditation, ministry). These biblical teachings equip us to experience God's ordinary supernatural presence in worship, meditation, and ministry.

Seminary students will find help in integrating their academic study of the Bible and theology with spiritual formation and ministry. Pastors can use this material and the study questions for leadership training sessions. Campus ministry leaders can use this book for staff training. Bible studies and Christian education classes can use it for three or six week courses.

I thank my wife, Robin, who gave valuable help editing this manuscript.

The Appendix "A Vision for Renewal" surveys modern culture and provides context for the biblical theology presented here. May God bless you as you consider this vision and share it with others.

John Jefferson Davis
Andrew Mutch Professor of Theology
Gordon-Conwell Theological Seminary
Hamilton, Massachusetts

1

THREE CRUCIAL TEXTS FOR SPIRITUAL RENEWAL

Acts 2, Matthew 28, John 17

THIS CHAPTER PROVIDES IMPORTANT new insights for personal growth and church renewal from three of the most important chapters in the Bible: Acts 2: Pentecost and the arrival of the Spirit; Matthew 28: the Great Commission and discipleship; and John 17: Jesus' great prayer for the unity of the church. The teachings in these texts are essential foundations for experiencing power in the Christian's life and success in the church's ministry.

Lives Changed by the Holy Spirit: The Apostle Peter

Before Pentecost, Peter discouraged Jesus from going to the cross, and in Gethsemane, he could not stay awake with Jesus for a single hour. He was afraid of the high priest's servant girl, denied his Master three times, and deserted Jesus after his arrest.

After Jesus rose from the dead, he breathed on Peter and the other disciples and imparted the Holy Spirit to them (John 20:22). Peter's life was dramatically changed after being filled with the Holy Spirit on the day of Pentecost (Acts 2:4). Peter powerfully proclaimed the death and resurrection of Jesus to the crowds assembled in Jerusalem. Three thousand were converted in a single day (Acts 2:41). What a remarkable difference a conscious experience of the Spirit's presence made in Peter's service to Christ!

Acts 2: Church the Way It Was Meant to Be—And Still Can Be Today

Consider the events on the day of Pentecost (Acts 2:1–41), and the remarkable, Spirit-empowered life of the early Jerusalem church that followed (Acts 2:42–46). Pentecost can be viewed from four simultaneous perspectives: earthly, heavenly, external, and internal.

First, the events of Pentecost on earth seen from an external point of view—from the point of view of those gathered in Jerusalem. The believers were together in one place and heard the sound of a violent wind filling the house. They saw flames of fire resting on each of them. Being filled with the Spirit, they began to speak in other languages, proclaiming the mighty acts of God (Acts 2:1–4). The flames of fire signified a new Mount Sinai, the inauguration of a new covenant, and God's real presence with his people.

In the old covenant fire was a visible sign that the LORD, the holy God of Israel, was present.[1] When the LORD called Moses to lead his people from bondage in Egypt, he appeared at Sinai, speaking from within the flames of fire in the burning bush (Exod 3:2, 4). At the exodus, the LORD was in the pillar of cloud by day and the pillar of fire by night, leading his people across the Red Sea and on to Sinai. The LORD descended on Mount Sinai in fire and called Moses to the top of the mountain to declare his covenant with his people (Exod 19:18, 20). At the dedication of the tabernacle the LORD filled it with his glory (Exod 40:34). During their wilderness travels the LORD continued to manifest his holy presence and to lead the people with the cloud by day and with fire in the cloud by night (Exod 40:36, 38). When Solomon dedicated the temple in

2

Jerusalem, the temple was filled with God's glory (1 Kgs 8:10, 11), signifying the LORD's real presence with his people.

The fire—an outward manifestation of God's glory and a sign of God's presence—was an Old Testament anticipation of the New Testament's good news of the gospel of Jesus, who is Emmanuel, "God with us." God dwelt in the midst of his people, giving them a visual sign of his presence. This awareness of God's presence was a distinctive mark of Israel's identity. Moses asked God, "How will anyone know that you are pleased with me and with your people unless you go with us? What else will distinguish me and your people from all the other people on the face of the earth?" (Exod 33:16). They knew they were a distinctive people because they knew they had been given distinctive, felt experiences—through sights, sounds, and miracles—of God's supernatural presence. Many Christian churches today lack felt experiences of God's presence, and consequently have lost the mark that distinguishes them from the surrounding culture and from other religions.

Because of their later persistent covenant disobedience and idolatry, the people of Israel lost their experience of the LORD's presence and glory. Ezekiel saw a vision of the divine glory departing from the temple (Ezek 10:18). God deserted his house on Mount Zion, anticipating the temple's coming destruction in 586 BC. God himself was going into exile with his people.

This was not to be the end of the story of God's presence with his people, however. The prophets had announced the good news that the LORD and his glory-fire would one day return to Jerusalem and to a new temple. Isaiah foresaw a day when the glory and fire of God would cover a righteous remnant gathered on Mount Zion: "Then the LORD will create over all of Mount Zion and over those who assemble there a cloud of smoke by day and a glow of flaming fire by night" (Isa 4:5). Zechariah prophesied that the LORD would return and be a wall of fire around Jerusalem and be her glory within (Zech 2:5). Ezekiel and Haggai both looked forward to a new temple that would again be filled with the divine glory (Ezek 43:5; Hag 2:7). Joel foresaw the time when God's Spirit

3

would be poured out on all people and fire poured out on earth (Joel 2:28–30).

These prophecies and others were fulfilled on the day of Pentecost. Ezekiel and Daniel had seen visions of God's heavenly throne flaming with fire (Ezek 1:4–5, 26–27; Dan 7:9). The fire surrounding the LORD's heavenly throne was now present on earth. The heavenly throne of God, now shared by Jesus, came down to earth in fire on Mount Zion, just as the LORD had earlier come down in fire on Mount Sinai. God called to Moses from within the burning bush, yet warned him not to come near (Exod 3:2–5). At Pentecost the newly born church was taken inside the burning bush, as it were, closer to God in the new covenant than even Moses had been in the old covenant when he was first called. When in the wilderness seventy elders were being ordained to help Moses and to be anointed with the Spirit, Moses expressed the wish that "all the LORD's people were prophets and that the LORD would put his Spirit on them" (Num 11:29). What was granted to the few in the old covenant was granted to all in the new covenant. Moses's wish was fulfilled on Pentecost, when all were filled with the Spirit and prophesied (Acts 2:18), proclaiming God's mighty acts in the resurrection and exaltation of Jesus as Messiah and LORD.

Second, consider the events of Pentecost from a heavenly and internal perspective—Jesus' own experience in heaven on the day of Pentecost. Sermons on Acts 2 typically focus on what the early church experienced on earth or on what the modern church would like to experience. But the early church's experience—and anyone's today—is grounded in what Jesus first experienced in heaven. The firstborn Son, Jesus, exalted in heaven, was the first to experience the promise to sons and daughters in Joel 2:28–29:

> I will pour out my Spirit on all people.
> Your sons and daughters will prophesy . . .
> Even on my servants, both men and women,
> I will pour out my Spirit in those days.

Jesus was the first of these sons and servants to receive the promised Spirit. As Peter declared: "Being exalted to the right hand of

4

the Father, he has received from the Father the promised Holy Spirit and has poured out what you now see and hear" (Acts 2:33). At his exaltation in heaven at the completion of his earthly ministry, Jesus received from his Father, in greater fullness and joy, the same Spirit he had received in humility at his baptism, at the beginning of his ministry. The Father who was well pleased with his beloved Son at the beginning of his ministry was joyously pleased with his Son at its completion. The Spirit who empowered Jesus on earth was given to him in even greater fullness in heaven. He was Spirit-baptized twice—first through John on earth, then by his Father in heaven.

In Hebrews 2:12, the writer states that Jesus was fulfilling in heaven Psalm 22:22, prophesying in heaven:[2] "I will declare your name to my brothers; in the presence of the congregation I will sing your praises." On the day of Pentecost, Jesus, who was also fulfilling Joel 2:28 ("your sons will prophesy"), was the first of the sons who was "prophesying"—giving praise to the Father. Jesus was—and still is—leading the heavenly worship. The praises of the church below (Acts 2:4, 11) were—and still are—a Spirit-empowered participation in Jesus' anointed worship above, his prophesying.

Peter's quotation of Joel 2:28–32 in Acts 2 and his application of it to Jesus is also evidence for the deity of Christ. The Joel text that promises that the LORD, the God of Israel, would pour out the Spirit, was applied by the inspired Peter to Jesus. What the text promised that the LORD would do, Jesus did: he poured out the Spirit. Joel 2:28–32, and its inspired commentary in Acts 2:33, is striking evidence of the New Testament writers' ascription of deity to Christ.[3] Acts 2 shows that New Testament Christology was high from the start—not a later development in the early church.[4]

Joel 2:28–32 is not the only Old Testament text that Jesus experienced on the day of Pentecost. He also experienced the fulfillment of Psalm 110 and Psalm 16. He was exalted to the Father's right hand (Ps 110:1) where he now reigns, awaiting the subduing of all his enemies beneath his feet. The Father did not abandon him to the grave or leave his body to decay (Acts 2:27 = Ps 16:10),

5

but raised him from the dead by the Spirit and filled him with joy in his presence (Acts 2:27 = Ps 16:11). Jesus was the first to experience powerful, positive emotions on the day of Pentecost. He was happy and full of joy because he was in his happy Father's presence, and he shared that joy with his people below.

Luke's account in Acts 2 of Jesus' receiving the Spirit in heaven above and the church's receiving the Spirit on earth below pictures what churches can experience today. With Christ we were raised from the dead and seated with Christ in the heavenly places (Eph 2:5, 6). In Christ we share Jesus' joy in the presence of the Father. We can testify to the mighty acts of God—Jesus' resurrection and exaltation. We, like Peter on the day of Pentecost, can understand in a deeper way the Old Testament messianic prophecies, now illuminated by the Spirit.

Dwight L. Moody:
A Deeper Experience of the Holy Spirit

Dwight L. Moody was one of history's greatest evangelists. He was already a successful pastor and evangelist when he traveled to New York in 1871 to raise money for those who had suffered loss in the recent Chicago fire. God placed on Moody's heart a longing for a deeper experience of the presence, love, and power of the Holy Spirit. He describes what happened to him as follows:

> I was crying all the time that God would fill me with his Spirit. Well, one day in the city of New York—oh, what a day! I cannot describe it, I seldom refer to it; it is almost too sacred an experience to name. . . . I can only say that God revealed himself to me, and I had such an experience of His love that I had to ask him to stay his hand. I went to preaching again. The sermons were not different; I did not present any new truths; and yet hundreds were converted. I would not now be placed back where I was before that blessed experience if you should give me all the world.

Moody's deeper experience of the Holy Spirit did not involve any spectacular outward manifestations such as tongues, miracles, or healing, but rather a new awareness of the Spirit's presence, flooding his soul with the love of God. Moody was a changed man. His evangelistic work became worldwide. By the time he died as many as 100 million people may have heard the gospel through Moody.

What effect did the outpouring of the Spirit have on the early Jerusalem church? Acts 2:42–46 depicts what our churches can experience today:

> They devoted themselves to the apostles' teaching and to the fellowship, to the breaking of bread and to prayer. Everyone was filled with awe, and many wonders and miraculous signs were done by the apostles. All the believers were together and had everything in common. Selling their possessions and goods, they gave to anyone as he had need. Every day they continued to meet together in the temple courts. They broke bread in their homes and ate together with glad and sincere hearts, praising God and enjoying the favor of all the people. And the Lord added to their number daily those who were being saved.

Luke describes a quality of church life possible for us today. The Spirit's presence and power was intended by God to last throughout church history. The day of Pentecost marked the ending of a centuries-long drought when the Holy Spirit had seemed to be absent from the lives of God's people.

Acts 2 describes the beginning, not the ending of the Spirit's empowering presence. The day of Pentecost was not a "one and done" giving of the Spirit. The Spirit was given because Jesus had been raised to the Father's right hand (Acts 2:33). Jesus is still exalted at the Father's right hand; his position has not changed. Jesus promised that he would send another Counselor, the Holy Spirit, to be with the church forever: "I will ask the Father and he will give you another Counselor to be with you forever" (John 14:16). Jesus promised that the Spirit would be present forever, not only in the apostolic age. The promise of the Spirit's continuing presence has no expiration date; the new life in the Spirit lasts into eternity.

Jesus' promise of the Spirit's "forever" presence gathered together many Old Testament prophecies about the return of the Spirit. God would pour out the Spirit on all his people (Joel 2:28–32; Ezek 39:29); guard Jerusalem with a ring of fire (Zech 2:5); shelter a faithful remnant on Mount Zion under the glory cloud (Isa 4:5); and fill a new temple with his glory (Hag 2:7).

The book of Acts shows that the Spirit's arrival on the day of Pentecost was not a one-time, temporary event. Believers were filled with the Spirit both on the day of Pentecost (Acts 2:4), and also on subsequent occasions. Peter was filled again with the Spirit when he testified before the Sanhedrin (Acts 4:8). The believers were filled again with the Spirit after Peter and John were released from prison (Acts 4:31). The first deacons were known to be "full of the Spirit" (Acts 6:3). Stephen was full of grace and power and spoke powerfully by the Spirit (Acts 6:10). The Samaritans received the Spirit after Peter and John prayed for them (Acts 8:17). Shortly after his conversion, Paul's sight was restored and he was filled with the Spirit through the laying on of hands by Ananias (Acts 9:17). Cornelius and his household received the Spirit while Peter was still preaching the gospel to them (Acts 10:44, 45). After the disciples of John the Baptist in Ephesus were baptized and Paul laid hands on them, they received the Spirit and spoke in tongues (Acts 19:5, 6).

The continuation of the Spirit's presence—not the Spirit's absence—is clearly taught in the Pauline Epistles. For Paul the baptism of the Holy Spirit was the initial experience of all new believers: "For we were all baptized by one Spirit into one body . . . and we were all given the one Spirit to drink" (1 Cor 12:13). For Paul, the filling of the Spirit is a subsequent and ongoing experience: "Keep on being filled with the Holy Spirit" (*pleirousthe en pneumati*: present passive imperative; Eph 5:18; author's translation). Christ and the Father intend the Spirit to keep filling the church until the whole body is fully mature and united (Eph 4:13).

This continued giving of the Spirit reflects God's amazing goodness and generosity to his people. As God says through Jeremiah, "I will make an everlasting covenant with them: I will never stop doing good to them . . . I will rejoice in doing them good . . . with all my heart and soul" (Jer 32:40, 41). This is one of the most emphatic statements in Scripture of God's warm, positive feelings for his children. This text describes not only God's actions of blessing us, but also God's feelings when blessing us. God experiences wholehearted enjoyment in blessing us, and he intends to enjoy blessing us for all eternity!

Acts 2:42–46 presents four priorities and six marks for Spirit-empowered churches. Four priorities in the Jerusalem church were devotion to 1) the apostles' teaching (*didache*); 2) fellowship (*koinonia*); 3) breaking of bread (*eucharistia*); and 4) prayer (*proseuche*). Teaching and prayer were important for the community both before (Acts 1:2, 3, 14) and after Pentecost (Acts 2:42). In the forty days between the resurrection and the ascension, Jesus spoke to the apostles about the kingdom of God (Acts 1:3) as he had in his earlier ministry. Luke specifically states that this teaching was "through the Holy Spirit" (Acts 1:2).

Jesus was giving the disciples—and us—an important example of doing ministry in the *ordinary supernatural* power of the Spirit. During this forty-day period Jesus was not casting out demons, healing people, turning water into wine, or raising people from the dead. In this final opportunity to train the disciples, Jesus' focus was not on miraculous manifestations of the Spirit, but on the quieter but crucially important ministry of the Spirit to give knowledge and understanding of the truth. Because of the presence of the Spirit, the apostles were able to understand and to remember Jesus' message better than they had before. In the final analysis, sound doctrine and biblical teaching can be more valuable to God's kingdom than miraculous healings—though God still gives miracles today—because healings can be temporary, while biblical truth and godly character last into eternity.

Ministry should not be done in natural ability alone—human energy, knowledge, and credentials (Level 1)—but also as enhanced by the ordinary supernatural work of the Spirit, accessed in prayer (Level 2); and, if God sovereignly grants, in the extraordinary supernatural energy of miracles, signs, and wonders (Level 3). There are three levels (natural; ordinary supernatural; extraordinary supernatural) at which ministry can be performed, not just two (natural or supernatural). Some churches and pastors do not adequately recognize and practice the intermediate level of the ordinary supernatural, and assume that if miracles are not happening, the supernatural power of God is not present. But the ordinary supernatural actions of the Spirit—illumination of the Scriptures, preaching that actually changes lives, conviction of sin leading to repentance and obedience, the fruit of the Spirit, and the formation of godly character—are the very heart and soul of ministry. Through faith, prayer, and fresh anointings of the Spirit, natural abilities and human energy can be enhanced and lifted up to the level of the ordinary supernatural, producing results that last into eternity. If ministry is done only in the power of the natural, teaching and preaching can be biblically accurate and doctrinally correct, and yet produce no lasting fruit. The fruit of the Holy Spirit cannot be produced by our human spirit and natural abilities, but only by the divine and (ordinary) supernatural action of the Holy Spirit.

The importance of prayer was shown in the extended prayer meeting before Pentecost: "They all joined together constantly in prayer" (Acts 1:14). This text indicates that the disciples spent extended time in prayer, that all were involved, and that their minds and intentions were united in prayer. The term used in this verse, *homothumadon,* means "of one mind." Most prayer meetings today do not combine these three elements: all in the church attending; spending extensive amounts of time in corporate prayer; and being of "one mind," in spiritual alignment. These three elements of serious prayer have characterized virtually every great revival in church history. Such prayer in the ordinary supernatural (Acts 1:14) was the gateway to the extraordinary filling of all the church with the Spirit on Pentecost (Acts 2:4). Before all were filled with the Spirit, all were praying persistently and unitedly, waiting for the arrival of the Spirit and power promised by Jesus (Acts 1:4, 5, 8). In the days following Pentecost, the apostles continued to give their attention to prayer and the ministry of the word (Acts 6:4).[5]

The breaking of bread (Acts 2:42) signifies the frequent, even daily (Acts 2:46) sharing of meals together. The Jerusalem church continued with one another the table fellowship that the first disciples had enjoyed with Jesus.[6] This may have involved both agape or fellowship meals and the Eucharist or Lord's Supper.

These common meals were signs of the ongoing fellowship inaugurated by the arrival of the Spirit and the new covenant. They were signs of life in the Spirit. The fellowship of these early believers was more than casual conversation over a cup of coffee in the church fellowship hall. This fellowship was an experience of a new quality of life given by the Spirit—a sharing in the life of the Trinity. As the apostle John came to realize, the fellowship of Christians with one another was not only a human relationship: "Our fellowship is with the Father and his Son, Jesus Christ" (1 John 1:3). John wrote to invite others into that fellowship, so that joy might be complete (1 John 1:4).

All four priorities of the Spirit-filled Jerusalem church— apostolic teaching, fellowship, breaking of bread together, and prayer—were critical to the vitality and power of the church. These priorities have, in varying degrees, characterized every great renewal movement in church history. These priorities are foundational for church revitalization today.

Acts 2:42–46 presents six marks describing what God intended for the New Testament church. The first mark is a sense of awe: "Everyone was filled with awe," (lit., *fear; phobos,* Acts 2:43). The word *awesome* is overused. But in the context of the early Jerusalem church, *awesome* was quite accurate. *Awe* suggests a state of mind that lifts our consciousness above the everyday range of our usual emotions. One definition of *awe* is "reverent wonder with a touch of fear inspired by the grand or sublime."[7]

Awe is the proper human response to the grandeur, power, holiness, and majesty of God. When God descended on Mount Sinai in thunder, lightning, and fire, "everyone in the camp trembled"

11

(Exod 19:16). In Isaiah's famous temple vision the prophet saw the Holy One of Israel "high and lifted up," and was overcome with a sense of his own unworthiness and sin in the presence of God (Isa 6).

When Peter, James, and John saw the glory of Jesus' divine nature on the Mount of Transfiguration, they were afraid (Mark 9:6). Such fear is an appropriate human reaction to a close encounter with God's majesty and holiness.

The experience of awe was not limited to the early Jerusalem church. The apostle Paul could refer to the palpable sense that the "power of the Lord Jesus is present" when Jesus' name was invoked by the gathered assembly in Corinth (1 Cor 5:4). Paul could assume, without lengthy explanation, that his readers in Corinth would understand his meaning experientially.

The author of Hebrews understood Christian worship as a supernatural encounter: "You have come to Mount Zion, to the heavenly Jerusalem, to the city of the living God. You have come to thousands upon thousands of angels in joyful assembly" (Heb 12:22). The author reminded his readers to worship God with "reverence and awe, for our God is a consuming fire" (Heb 12:28). The church needs to rediscover this sense of the awesomeness of the holy God—the God who promises to come into our midst as we gather in his name (1 Cor 5:4; Matt 18:20).

A second mark of the early church were signs and wonders done through the apostles (Acts 2:43b). Powerful works of healing and exorcism were common in early Christianity. These demonstrations of spiritual power were significant elements in the church's growth.[8] Jesus promised his followers that anyone who believed in him would do the works he was doing: "I tell you the truth, anyone who has faith in me will do what I have been doing" (John 14:12). Not just the twelve apostles, but seventy-two others were sent out to proclaim the kingdom of God, to heal, and to cast out demons (Luke 10:1, 9, 17). In Paul's list of spiritual gifts, the gift of miracles (1 Cor 12:9, 28) is distinct from the gift of apostle (1 Cor 12:28) and not tied integrally to it. All apostles had the gift of miracles, but not all who had the gift of miracles were apostles. There is no compelling reason, theologically, that signs and wonders should be absent in churches today. Examples of such spiritual power are widely attested in many majority-world churches outside Europe and North America.[9]

A third mark of life in the Spirit-empowered Jerusalem church was generous unity (Acts 2:44–45). Luke states that the believers were together, selling their possessions, holding them in common, and giving to other members of the community as they had need. While it is true that the way this unity was expressed—everyone selling their possessions—proved to be temporary, it is still true that God intended for unity and generosity to be continuing signs of Christian life in the Spirit. Unity and generosity are rooted in the character of God and should be reflected in the body of Christ. Such unity and generosity contributed significantly to the growth of the early church.

A fourth mark of early Christian congregations was ministry taking place outside religious buildings, the temple and synagogues. The believers met together for fellowship and worship not only in the temple courts but also in private homes (Acts 2:46). After the third and fourth centuries, when Christianity became a legally sanctioned religion, Christian activity became increasingly located in the sacred spaces of church buildings. This pattern has continued down to the present. Revitalized Christian ministries today need to recapture this early spiritual dynamic, when Christian ministry and fellowship were not limited to church buildings on one day of the week but were experienced in the marketplace and in homes on the other six days of the week.[10]

A fifth mark is found in Acts 2:47: "enjoying the favor of all the people." The quality of life and joyful, harmonious relationships evident internally in the community were also evident externally to those outside. This attractive quality of life created favorable impressions of the early Christian movement and its adherents. Outsiders noticed the differences that the message of Jesus and the experience of the Spirit made in the lives of their Christian friends and neighbors.

In the United States today, many identified as evangelicals do not "enjoy the favor of all the people" but are perceived in a negative light. The research of Kinnaman and Lyons[11] found that many Americans believe that the movement had become too political, being identified with one political party.

The fifth mark led naturally to a sixth: natural, organic growth. "The Lord added to their number daily those who were being saved" (Acts 2:47). As Alan Kreider has shown in his seminal study *The Patient Ferment of the Early Church*, the Christian movement did not experience its remarkable growth because of organized evangelistic campaigns or seeker-sensitive worship services, but rather because of the depth of its worship, the intensive and extensive quality of its discipleship and membership practices, and the remarkable quality of the care that Christians provided for one another.[12] In this post-Christendom period of history, rediscovering and practicing these priorities of the pre-Constantinian church can provide the revitalization that is much needed by today's church.

Matthew 28: Doing Discipleship Jesus' Way

Then Jesus came to them and said, "All authority in heaven and earth has been given to me. Therefore go and make disciples of all nations, baptizing them in the name of the Father and of the Son and of the Holy Spirit, and teaching them to obey everything I have commanded you. And surely I am with you always, to the very end of the age" (Matt 28:18–20).

Matthew 28 Comes Alive: My Calling to Seminary

The year after my graduation from Duke University I taught high school math. I was invited to be an adult chaperone for a Campus

14

Crusade (now Cru) conference for high school students in Winter Park, Florida. On one of the final evenings of the conference, the speaker, whose name I do not remember, gave a message on the Great Commission (Matt 28:18-20). I sensed that God was speaking to me through that message, that I was being called to make disciples, and to prepare to do so by going to seminary. On the recommendation of friends in the Duke InterVarsity chapter, I decided to apply to Gordon Divinity School in Wenham, Massachusetts—a school I had never visited.

Hearing this message was an experience of the ordinary supernatural work of the Holy Spirit, illuminating the Scriptures, and motivating me to respond. This message altered the direction of my life, leading me to seminary, meeting my wife, Robin, and beginning a lifelong career of training seminarians in Christian doctrine—part of the task of making disciples for Jesus Christ.

Today's churches need a new paradigm of discipleship. The primary focus of discipleship needs to be shifted from teaching Bible knowledge to teaching obedience to Jesus' commands. The point is not that Bible knowledge is unimportant. The point is rather that Bible knowledge is not an end in itself, but a means to the end of obedience and conformity to the character of Christ.

Changed Lives: Jasmine Hears the Voice of God

Jasmine (not her real name) was a sophomore at Wellesley College and caught in the middle of a major personal crisis. She went to the lower level of the college library to study, and there, alone, heard a voice saying, "It will be all right." She was not a believer at the time. She returned to her dorm room, where to her amazement she learned that the crisis had been resolved. She became involved in the Wellesley Christian Fellowship and was taken to Park Street Church in Boston by her friends, who mentored her.

Jasmine began a lifelong journey of faith that has continued to the present day. In her liberal church background she had never heard it clearly taught that "Christ died for your sins . . . Jesus is God's only Son." Now, through the work of the Holy Spirit, she had come to understand these biblical truths in a personal and life-changing way.

This new paradigm recognizes that orthodoxy and Bible knowledge are not ends in themselves, but rather means to the ends of orthopraxy and Christlike character. Orthopraxy means obedience to the commands of Jesus. True conversion produces life changes that are visible and attractive to those outside the church. Before Christians attempt to transform culture, Christ must first transform Christians. The emphasis on obeying all that Jesus commanded requires a rediscovery of the labor-intensive discipleship employed in the pre-Constantinian church.[13]

Why a New Paradigm of Discipleship is Needed

Methods of discipleship effective in an earlier Christian America are less effective in our current culture. Rather than the churches transforming culture, the culture has transformed churches, with both church and culture becoming less Christian. In 1973, the Supreme Court legalized abortion across the United States. The year 2015 witnessed the Supreme Court's legalization of same-sex marriage and the emergence of transgenderism as a cutting edge of cultural change. Such decisions were signs of the marginalization of biblical standards for sexuality and marriage.

A recent study of the state of religion in America concluded that "no indicator of traditional religious belief or practice is going up . . . If there is a trend, it is toward less religion."[14] Growth rates for evangelical churches are generally flat. The growth that is occurring is due more to immigration than to evangelistic and church planting efforts. The percentage of "Nones" in the United States who claim no religious affiliation has been increasing and

16

is now approaching 20 percent.[15] Young people in their twenties show decreasing levels of interest in and loyalty to institutional churches.[16]

The political efforts of the Christian Right and the Moral Majority did little to stem the tide of moral change in America. These efforts produced a backlash against conservative Christians who were seen as imposing their religious standards on others. The neo-evangelical project of Ockenga, Henry, and Graham for renewing the mainline denominations has, for the most part, not succeeded. Mainline churches have continued to drift further away from biblical orthodoxy and continue to dwindle in membership.

These facts should provoke pastors and teachers to engage in fresh thinking about discipleship. The current paradigms and practices are simply not getting the job done.

New Readings of Discipleship: The Biblical Witness

The new paradigm of discipleship—focusing on obedience, not just knowledge—is consistent with the priorities of the Old Testament, Jesus, the apostles, and the early church. Through Old Testament prophets, God promised that he would make a new covenant with his people, a new covenant characterized by obedience: "I will put my law in their minds and write it on their hearts. I will be their God and they will be my people" (Jer 31:34). God's law "in their minds" would not merely be correct ideas about the law but God's law actually obeyed. God spoke of the new covenant through Ezekiel: "And I will put my Spirit in you and move you to follow my decrees and be careful to keep my laws" (Ezek 36:27).

For Jesus, making disciples meant training people to obey all his commands.[17] His commands are now internalized in the hearts of his disciples and embodied in intentional obedience. In contrast to theories of knowledge in the Enlightenment and modern science, in Jesus' theory of knowledge the practical reason of obedience is prior to the theoretical reason of bare cognition. "If anyone chooses to do God's will, he will find out whether my teaching comes from God or whether I speak on my own" (John

17

7:17). Disciples of Jesus do not reason their way into obedience; disciples of Jesus obey their way into understanding.

Jesus' epistemology of obedience is shared by his apostles. Paul stated that the primary aim of his apostolic mission to the Gentiles was to call them to the "obedience that comes from faith" (Rom 1:5). God's people must devote themselves to good deeds (Titus 3:14). John remembered that the essential sign of a true disciple was not correct creedal belief or saying "Lord, Lord," but rather, obeying Jesus' command to love others as Jesus loved them. "By this all men will know that you are my disciples, if you love one another" (John 13:34, 35). John stated, "We know that we have come to know him if we obey his commands" (1 John 2:3). James knew that a faith that has no deeds of obedience does not save (Jas 1:14). True faith is demonstrated by what the disciple of Jesus does (Jas 2:18). Writing to new believers in Asia Minor who had "purified themselves by obeying the truth," Peter encouraged them to "love one another deeply from the heart" (1 Pet 1:22). True faith is demonstrated by Christlike behavior and character (2 Pet 1:5–8).

As Alan Kreider demonstrated in *The Patient Ferment of the Early Church*,[18] the church of the first four centuries focused on the formation of Christian character and obedient behavior. This meant extensive, lengthy catechesis and individual mentoring. The catechumen's behavior was changed by this process of formation in ways that intrigued and attracted outsiders, and the church grew as a result.

Discipleship Jesus' Way:
How It Faded in the Post-Constantinian Church

The early church's intensive catechetical program of inculcating the behaviors and attitudes mandated by Jesus began to fade after the fourth century. With the conversion of Constantine, growing numbers of outsiders began to seek entry into the church. The focus in catechesis began to shift away from embodied behavior and obedience, to correct belief as the primary mark of Christian identity. This shift may have been a reaction to the rise of heresies such as Arianism, Donatism, and Pelagianism.[19] By AD 600, infant baptism had become the norm in the West, with very few adult conversions in Europe. The practice of infant baptism, together with the belief in baptismal regeneration, meant that one became a Christian through this priestly act in church. Infants could not have a conscious experience of the reception of the Holy Spirit, typical of adult conversions in the pre-Constantinian period. Together with the virtual disappearance of extensive catechetical formation in the medieval period, these practices produced masses of nominal, poorly taught Christians.

The Reformers attempted to combat the weaknesses of medieval Roman Catholicism by emphasizing biblical doctrine and right administration of the sacraments. In catechesis, however, the Reformers did not substantially challenge the inherited emphasis on right belief rather than transformed behavior. The Reformers recovered the biblical doctrine of justification by faith alone but they did not sufficiently emphasize the New Testament's insistence on doing good works. Roman Catholic sacramentalism was largely replaced by Protestant "sermonism" that was overly optimistic in its expectation for what Bible teaching—in and of itself—could accomplish in transforming behavior.

In his 1792 *Enquiry into the Obligation of Christians to Use Means for the Conversion of the Heathen,* William Carey challenged the long-prevailing view that the Great Commission had been fulfilled by the original apostles and was no longer binding on the church. For much of the medieval and early modern periods, this text was read primarily for what it was thought to teach concerning the doctrine of the Trinity and the administration of baptism.[20] In his fresh reading of this text, Carey recovered the boundary-crossing aspects of the passage. Carey retrieved the missional dimensional of the Great Commission but did not emphasize the formational goal of Christ's mandate: obedience to all the commands of Jesus.

The history of revivalism since the First and Second Great Awakenings has also revealed some theological deficits in this stream of the evangelical tradition. The emphasis on making decisions for Christ shifted attention away from extensive, patient methods of discipleship to the born-again experience of regeneration. Regeneration can be instantaneous, but sanctification generally is not.[21] Babes in Christ can be conceived very quickly, but training mature disciples takes much time and effort.

Making Disciples Today

In light of biblical teachings and early church practice, how then should today's church make disciples? In addition to teaching Bible content and spiritual disciplines, church and seminary discipleship courses should give greater attention to character development as the early church did. Many seminary students and church members have family backgrounds that are dysfunctional in varying degrees. Many have attention spans distracted by social media, thought lives affected by internet pornography, and inner lives struggling with depression and anxiety. Substantial remediation is needed.

Seminaries and churches need to consider with new seriousness the character qualifications for church leaders specified in texts such as 1 Timothy 3:1-13 and Titus 1:5-9. Peter Scazzero's *Emotionally Healthy Spirituality* is helpful in dealing with issues of emotional woundedness. Ideally, not only courses in spiritual formation and discipleship, but every course in a seminary's curriculum or church's education program should be measured by Jesus' criteria of discipleship: training disciples who obey all Jesus' commands.

Local churches should adopt higher standards and expectations for membership. If the early church expected two or three years of catechesis before baptism and full membership, is it unreasonable to think of new members' classes that could be six months in duration? The pastor could function as the chief catechist, and each candidate for membership could be assigned a sponsor or mentor. These mentors could meet on a regular basis with the candidate for prayer, encouragement, and accountability. An extended study of the Gospel of Matthew, focusing on identifying, discussing, and applying all the commands of Jesus in this Gospel, could serve as the basis for such a catechetical curriculum.

Jesus warned his would-be followers not to say "Lord, Lord" and yet not "do what I say." On the other hand, those who hear his words and put them into practice are like wise builders who dig deep and build the foundation on rock (Luke 7:46–48). Their lives can then withstand the stresses and storms that surely come. The early church heeded these warnings, put them into practice, and grew as a result. Today's churches would do well to follow the good examples of these earliest disciples.

John 17: Rediscovering Unity as Integral to the Mission of Jesus

John 17 is one of the most important chapters in the Bible for the spiritual health of the church. In his high priestly prayer Jesus emphasized the unity of believers as essential both to his message and to his mission. In this great prayer, unparalleled in its theological depth, Jesus showed his concern not only for truth and correct belief but also for visible unity among his followers, a unity that would make his message credible to the world.

Jesus Prayed for Himself: John 17:1–5

Before his betrayal, arrest, and death on the cross, Jesus prayed for himself, manifesting his own unity with the Father. Several elements of his prayer are instructive for our Christian lives. Jesus first prayed, "Glorify your Son, so that your Son may glorify you." Jesus' constant aim was to bring glory to the Father, not to himself. He prayed for the paradoxical "glory" of suffering death on the cross, in obedience to the will of the Father.

The request "Glorify your Son" was not a selfish desire. Jesus sought the Father's glory, not his own: "Glorify your Son, *that your Son may glorify you*" (emphasis added). Jesus knew a fundamental truth: we can only give to others what God has first given to us.

Paul asked the Corinthians, who were boasting of their spiritual gifts, "What do you have that you did not receive? And if you did receive it, why do you boast as if you did not?" (1 Cor 4:7). Spiritual benefits we give others—wise counsel, heartfelt prayer, fresh insight—have first been given to us by the Spirit. Only the Spirit produces the Spirit's lasting fruit.

We are only partners with God in ministry, not primary agents. Even though Jesus in his divine nature had glory by right, the glory he was given on earth had first to be received from God. Jesus was constantly aware of his dependence on the Father. We too must constantly be aware that we are dependent on God for every good thought, word, or deed.

Growing into a fuller experience of salvation involves not only a deeper personal knowledge of Jesus, but also a deeper knowledge of the Father whom Jesus came to reveal. Jesus prayed for those who were to be given eternal life, that they "may know you, the only true God, and Jesus Christ whom you have sent" (John 15:3). A Jesus-only understanding and experience of God is incomplete. Both Jesus and Paul taught that full knowledge of God is a knowledge of the Father, through the Son, in the Spirit. Paul prayed that those in his churches would be given the Spirit of wisdom and revelation by the "glorious Father," in order that they might know him better (Eph 1:17).

A study by the Baylor Institute for Studies of Religion found that almost three-quarters of American adults had negative images and beliefs about God: images of an angry, critical, or distant God. Only about one-fourth had views of God that were predominantly benevolent.[22] Jesus, however, taught that the true God, his "Abba, Father," is the God whose character is portrayed in the fifteenth chapter of Luke's Gospel. This Father is like a good shepherd or a woman householder who seeks the lost and rejoices in finding his lost sheep or her lost coin. The Father known by Jesus is the father of the prodigal son who embraces the returning lost son with compassion and joy. Living in a society with so much family brokenness, Christians today need to meditate on Jesus' very positive images of God in order to be healed, and to experience more joyful relationships with all three persons of the Trinity.

Another notable element of Jesus' prayer for himself is the remarkable statement, "I have brought you glory on earth by completing the work you gave me to do" (John 17:4). How wonderful it would be to be able to say at the end of our lives, "Father, I have brought you glory on earth by finishing the work you gave me to do!" Many busy pastors and parents feel that their work is never done or done well enough. Jesus had a clear sense of the work that the Father had given him. His to-do list was not primarily determined by what other people or his own disciples wanted him to do. Jesus did not fulfill the common Jewish expectations for a good messiah. He did not heal all the sick, feed all the hungry, deliver all the demon-afflicted, or free the nation from the Romans.

How did Jesus discern the specific tasks the Father had given him? John's Gospel gives us answers. Before Jesus acted, he first looked to see what the Father was doing, as he did in healing the paralytic at the Bethesda Pool in Jerusalem (John 5:19). In his teaching and preaching ministry, he first listened in private to the Father before speaking in public in the Father's name: "I speak just what the Father has taught me" (John 8:28). Before leading others in ministry, he first followed the Spirit in preparation: "Jesus, full of the Holy Spirit . . . was led by the Spirit in the desert" (Luke 4:1). Before commanding his disciples to obey his commands, Jesus first obeyed his Father's commands: "If you obey my commands, you will remain in my love just as I have obeyed my Father's commands and remain in his love" (John 15:10). If we do what Jesus did in his relationship with the Father, we too will hear at the end of our days, "Well done, my good and faithful servant!"

Jesus Prayed for the Apostles: John 17:6–19

In John 17:6–19, Jesus prayed for the apostles; his prayer reveals that unity is foundational for successful mission to the world. Jesus prayed that his apostles would display a unity among themselves that reflected his own unity with the Father. This unity is comprehensive, involving a volitional unity of will and purpose, an emotional unity of shared joy, and a cognitive unity of shared belief and understanding.

Jesus prayed that the Father would protect his apostles by the power of his name, in order that "they may be one as we are one." This unity is based on a unity both of will and of purpose. Just as Jesus' will was aligned with the Father's in obedience to the Father's commands, so the apostles' wills were to be aligned with Jesus' will in obedience to his commands. Just as Jesus' purpose was to seek the Father's glory rather than his own, so should our purposes be to seek the glory of the Father and the Son, not our own.[23] Jesus prayed that the Father would protect the apostles from the designs of Satan, the evil one (17:15), who would seek to undermine such unity.

Jesus wanted the apostles to have "the full measure of my joy within them" (John 17:13). Just as Jesus experienced joy in the presence of the Father (Luke 10:21), we too can experience joy in the presence of Christ, united to him in the Spirit. This ordinary supernatural joy in the Spirit can prevail even in the face of the world's hatred and opposition: "I have given them your word, and the world has hated them" (John 17:14). This joy commends Jesus' message to the world and attracts those outside to the life of the Spirit-filled church (Acts 2:46–47).

Encountering God, Experiencing Joy: Blaise Pascal

Blaise Pascal was a brilliant French mathematician who helped lay the foundations of modern probability theory. He was also a devout Christian whose book *Penseés* is considered a religious classic. After his death in 1662, a piece of paper was discovered sewn inside his coat. It read as follows:

> From about half past ten in the evening to about half
> an hour after midnight. Fire. God of Abraham, God of
> Isaac, God of Jacob; Not the God of philosophers and

24

scholars. Absolute Certainty: Beyond reason. Joy. Peace.
Forgetfulness of the world and everything but God. The
world has not known thee, but I have known thee. Joy!
Joy! Joy! tears of joy!

Pascal had experienced a deep personal encounter with the God of
Abraham, Isaac, and Jacob and felt a profound joy that can only be
found in the presence of Christ and the living God. Such an experience of joy made God seem more real to Pascal. People today can
have an encounter with God and feel profound joy as well.

In John 17:17 Jesus prayed for the cognitive unity of the
apostles: "Sanctify them by the truth; your word is truth." Being
sanctified, set apart for God's service, involves agreement in shared
belief and understanding. The words of truth by which the apostles
were to be sanctified were the words that Jesus received from the
Father, then gave to them, and which they obeyed. Just as doctrinal
divisions among Christians throughout church history have been
a barrier to the credibility and spread of the gospel, so, too, unity
based on the teachings makes the message of Jesus more believable
to the world. This cognitive unity (truth), together with affective
(joy) and volitional unity (obedience), were Jesus' core priorities as
he prayed for the apostles and sent them in mission to the world.

Jesus Prayed for All of Us: John 17:20–26

Having prayed for his own unity with the Father and for the unity
of his disciples with one another, Jesus then prayed for the unity
of all later believers. Here we find profound expressions of Jesus'
understanding of his life, mission, and our salvation. Jesus prayed
that "all of them may be one, Father, just as you are in me and I
am in you. May they also be in us so that the world may believe
that you have sent me" (John 17:21). For what type of unity did
Jesus pray? This unity is not primarily outward, organizational, or
institutional. This unity is one that reflects the unity of the Father,
Son, and Spirit. Salvation itself is sharing in the life of the Trinity.[24]

This sharing in Jesus' life with the Father involves sharing in the glory that he received from the Father (John 17:22) and in the love that he continues to experience from the Father: "May they be brought to complete unity to let the world know that you . . . have loved them even as you have loved me" (John 17:23). This sharing in the common life of the Father, Son, and Spirit also means being indwelt by Jesus himself: "I have made you known to them . . . in order that the love you have for me may be in them and that I myself may be in them" (John 17:26).

The Holy Spirit, dwelling in us, connects Jesus' inner life with ours. Before our conversion, we had only an external relationship to Jesus, at best; he was outside us. At the human level, only with close friends in whose presence we feel safe and secure—not with outsiders or casual acquaintances—do we let down our hair and allow the other person to see our inner lives. After conversion, the Spirit gives us an insider relationship to Jesus, in which he shares his inner life—thoughts, feelings, plans—with us. We are not just servants, but friends: "I no longer call you servants, because a servant does not know his master's business. Instead, I have called you friends, for everything I have learned from my Father I have made known to you" (John 15:15).

At the human level, empathy creates a heart-to-heart connection between two people. At the spiritual level, the Holy Spirit creates a heart-to-heart connection between Jesus and us.[25] Human friends bond with one another through words, gestures, and facial expressions, communicating both verbally and non-verbally. The Holy Spirit bonds us with Jesus, communicating to us his thoughts and feelings—placing in our brains thoughts from God, and acting on our brains to create emotions that mirror the feelings Jesus has for us.

Sharing in the life of the Trinity means that in the Spirit, we are in the presence of the risen and glorified Christ, seeing his glory: "Father, I want those you have given me to be with me where I am and to see my glory" (John 17:24). We have a close-up view of Jesus' relationship with his Father. This beatific vision, to be experienced in its fullness in the age to come, is already available now.

The Spirit lifts us by faith into the heavenly places where we all can behold the glory of Christ (2 Cor 3:18).

When is Jesus' glorious vision of the unity of his followers to be realized? Is it a vision only realized in the age to come? Jesus gave his answer to this question of "When?" in John 14:20: "On that day [when the Spirit comes: 14:16] you will know [experientially] that I am in my Father, and that you are in me, and I am in you." The reception of the Spirit for the apostles was simultaneous with Pentecost. When the Spirit arrives for us, we are brought from an external relation to Jesus to an internal one of shared life and subjectivity. Believers after the resurrection and Pentecost can begin to live into the life in the Trinity, even though they do not yet experience that life in its fullness.

Finally, what would Jesus' vision of unity among his followers look like in the life of a local church? We have previously considered Luke's concrete picture of this unity in the second chapter of the book of Acts. Here believers, after a period of extensive, united corporate prayer (Acts 1:14), were all filled with the Spirit (Acts 2:4), and experienced worship and fellowship characterized by joy, generosity, and the awareness of God's presence (Acts 2:43–46). Their community life attracted those outside into their fellowship (Acts 2:47). This same experience of a supernaturally produced unity is still possible and available to today—to all who are willing to believe and to pray for it.

In this chapter we have studied three crucial texts vital for personal and church renewal: Acts 2, Matthew 28, and John 17. In the next chapter we study three crucial biblical truths: the Trinity, union with Christ, and the arrival of the Spirit.

Questions for Discussion:

1. Do you agree with the statement that the description of the life of the early Jerusalem church after the day of Pentecost in Acts 2:42–46 is how it should be for churches today? Why or why not? What feature of the life of the early church described

in Acts 2:42–46 would you most like to see strengthened in your church? What obstacles, if any, prevent your church from moving in that direction?

2. If you were discipled as a new Christian, what were the most important elements that you experienced in that discipleship? Has reading the material on Matthew 28 and the Great Commission changed or challenged your understanding of discipleship in any way? If you are a pastor, youth leader, or Bible study leader, what might you do differently in light of what you have read?

3. Which do you think is more important for the life of a local church: biblical truth or unity among believers? Which has been emphasized more in your church or parachurch experiences? Can you explain why Jesus teaches in John 17 that without visible unity among his followers, the world will not believe his message? Can you give examples from church history or your Christian experience why this could be true? What are some concrete steps pastors and churches in a given area could take to manifest to the community some significant signs of unity?

For further reading:

Alan Kreider, *The Patient Ferment of the Early Church: The Improbable Rise of Christianity in the Roman Empire.*

Shows how in-depth catechesis and discipleship were core elements in the growth of early Christian churches.

C. Peter Wagner, *Your Spiritual Gifts Can Help Your Church Grow.*

Practical helps on identifying and applying spiritual gifts in the local church.

John Wimber, *Power Evangelism: Signs and Wonders Today.*

Argues for the continuing validity of "signs and wonders" as accompaniments to the proclamation of the gospel today.

2

THREE CRUCIAL TEACHINGS FOR SPIRITUAL RENEWAL

Trinity, Union with Christ, and Arrival of the Spirit

THIS CHAPTER PRESENTS A vision for church renewal in a cultural context characterized as *post-Enlightenment, postcolonial,* and even *post-American.*[26] The term *post-Enlightenment* recognizes the need for greater critical distance from mindsets dominated by science, technology, and digital devices. *Postcolonial* recognizes that American churches are part of a global Christian movement in which the churches of Africa, Asia, and Latin America are now numerically dominant and in many cases more spiritually vibrant. *Post-American* suggests that American Christians should seek to live out more clearly the differences between their core values and the dominant values of secular culture: consumerism, entertainment, and competitive individualism.

Three biblical truths—the Trinity, union with Christ, and arrival of the Spirit—provide the basis upon which churches today can recover the early church's supernatural power. All three doctrines have practical applications for worship, personal spirituality, and ministry.

The Holy Spirit and Spiritual Power: Jonathan Edwards and the Great Awakening

Our gospel came to you not simply with words, but also . . .
with the Holy Spirit and deep conviction (1 Thess 1:5).

In his 1737 *Narrative of Surprising Conversions,* Jonathan Edwards described how the Holy Spirit was bringing many in New England to a deeper personal experience of the Christian doctrines they had previously believed:

> Converting influences very commonly brought an extraordinary conviction of the reality and certainty of the great things of religion. . . . Some are thus convinced of the truth of the gospel in general, and that the Scriptures are the word of God; others have their minds more fixed on some great doctrine of the gospel, some truths they are meditating upon or reading in Scripture. . . . The arguments are the same they have heard hundreds of times, but now their conviction of them is altogether new; they come with a new and before unexperienced power. . . . Before, they heard it was so; but now, they see it to be so indeed.

Like Job, those awakened by the Spirit in a personal encounter with the living God could say, "My ears had heard of you, but now my eyes have seen you" (Job 42:5).

Ultimate Reality: Doctrine of the Trinity[27]

1. Historical Overview

The doctrine of the Trinity is the most fundamental of all the doctrines of the Christian faith and expresses the distinctive Christian understanding of God. As Karl Barth has noted, the doctrine of the Trinity "is what basically distinguishes the Christian doctrine of God as Christian . . . in contrast to all other possible doctrines of God or concepts of revelation."[28] In spite of its critical importance, this doctrine is one of the least understood by many believers. Often it is perceived as having little practical significance for Christian living. It will be helpful to consider this teaching's historical development.

After several centuries of relative neglect, the doctrine of the Trinity experienced a renaissance in the twentieth century, largely due to the seminal contributions of Karl Barth and Karl Rahner.[29] Barth placed the doctrine of the Trinity at the beginning of his *Church Dogmatics*, recognizing it to be foundational for the Christian view of revelation and the entire fabric of Christian faith. Rahner attempted to reconnect the immanent and economic Trinity in his now widely known axiom, "The 'economic' Trinity is the 'immanent' Trinity and the 'immanent' Trinity is the 'economic' Trinity."[30] Rahner attempted to reconnect the Trinity more closely to the history of salvation and the biblical narrative. The renewed interest in the doctrine of the Trinity stimulated by Barth and Rahner has been expressed in the more recent work of theologians such as Jurgen Moltmann, Leonardo Boff, Thomas F. Torrance, Catherine LaCugna, John D. Zizioulas, and others.[31] Systematic theologians, philosophical theologians, and analytic philosophers have participated in this modern renewal of interest in the doctrine of the Trinity.[32]

The New Testament and early Christian church did not have an explicit doctrine of the Trinity. The basis, however, for later developments were contained in the church's recognition of the deity of Christ and the reception of the Holy Spirit after Pentecost. Baptismal texts such as Matthew 28:19, benedictions such as 2 Corinthians 13:14, and references to Christian salvation such as 1 Peter 1:1-2 express the triadic nature of Christian life and experience.[33] The Trinitarian patterns of New Testament revelation are found in evangelistic invitations to know the triune God (Acts 2:38-39); in references to salvation (Eph 2:18, 21-22; Rom 5:5-6);

in statements of assurance of salvation (Rom 8:14–17; Gal 3:3–6; 4:6); in references to intercessory prayer (Rom 15:30; Rom 8:26, 27); in the understanding of spiritual truths (1 Cor 2:12–13, 16); in the making of Christian disciples (Matt 28:19–20); and in the giving of spiritual gifts to the church (1 Cor 12:3–6).[34]

The classical formulation of the doctrine of the Trinity was achieved in the wake of the Arian controversy at the Council of Constantinople in 381, reflecting the seminal contributions of the Cappadocian fathers: Basil of Caesarea, Gregory of Nyssa, and Gregory of Nazianzus.[35] As a result of their theological work the full deity of the Holy Spirit was affirmed and Trinitarian terminology was clarified and standardized. The term *ousia* (Latin, *substantia*) was used to refer to the nature or essence common to the three, and *hypostasis* (Latin, *persona*) to refer to the three distinct persons in the Godhead: Father, Son, and Holy Spirit.

In the Latin West, Augustine's treatise *On the Trinity* set the pattern for almost all later theological reflections on the topic. Augustine argued that the unity of knowledge, memory, and will[36] in the human person reflected the unity of the three divine persons. Some later critics saw such comparisons as verging on modalism, undercutting the real distinctions in God. Augustine's notion that the three persons were relations within the divine nature was further developed by Thomas Aquinas.[37] Aquinas attempted to clarify the distinctions among the three, but with the unintended consequence that the persons were depersonalized—at least from the point of view of a common-sense understanding of the term *person*.[38] Aquinas's placement of the doctrine of the Trinity after his discussion of the One God and his existence and attributes—a decision followed by many subsequent theologians—had the unintended consequence of deemphasizing the Trinity as the distinctive Christian and biblical understanding of God.

An important development in the West's Trinitarian theology arose in the medieval period in the *filioque* controversy. In the sixth century, the Western church added the phrase "and from the Son" (*filioque*) to the Nicene Creed, changing the original wording that the Son "proceeds from the Father."[39] Some scholars have suggested that the West was concerned to emphasize the full deity of the Son, as reflected in his full co-agency in the procession of the Spirit.

The Eastern church objected and continues to object to the Western addition on both procedural and theological grounds. From the Eastern point of view, the West had no right to amend an ecumenical creed, and theologically, the Western "double procession" view is believed to undercut the unity of the Godhead, which in the Eastern understanding is grounded in the person of the Father. The issue is still a divisive one between the East and the West.

In the Reformation period, Luther, Calvin, and the English Reformers did not propose new constructive developments in Trinitarian doctrine. Their energies focused on doctrines of more immediate concern, such as justification and the sacraments.[40] In the Enlightenment and modern periods the doctrine of the Trinity suffered an eclipse, with Schleiermacher relegating it to the end of his treatise, *The Christian Faith*. Schleiermacher claimed to find no basis in religious experience for "the original and eternal existence of distinctions within the Divine Essence."[41] Unitarians and other rationalist critics abandoned the doctrine altogether. The modern renewal of Trinitarian theology initiated by Barth and Rahner can be seen as a response to the challenges to the tradition that were posed by Schleiermacher and Enlightenment critics.

Wesley's Fetter Lane Experience: Experiencing the Joy and Majesty of God's Presence

On January 1, 1739, John Wesley recorded in his diary his remarkable experience of joy in God's presence at the London Moravian Fetter Lane Society's watch night prayer meeting:

> Mr. Hall, Hinching, Ingham, Whitefield, Hutching, and my brother Charles were present at our love feast in Fetter Lane with about sixty of our brethren. About three in the morning as we were continuing in prayer, the power

> of God came mightily upon us so much that many cried out for exceeding joy and many fell to the ground. As soon as we were recovered a little from that awe and amazement at the presence of His majesty, we broke out with one voice, "We praise Thee, O God, we acknowledge Thee to be the Lord."

This unexpected experience of God's majestic presence, during extended corporate prayer, led to spontaneous words of praise and thanksgiving, using the words of the ancient Christian prayer, the *Te Deum*. The triune God had been revealed in a powerful way in their Christian experience.

---

3. Doctrine of the Trinity: Historical Understandings

The following exposition summarizes the orthodox doctrine of the Trinity, as based in the biblical witness and developed in the historic creeds of the churches.[42] The following three statements express teachings accepted in both the Western and Eastern branches of the church.

1. There is one true God and only one true God.
2. This one God exists eternally in three distinct persons: Father, Son, and Holy Spirit.
3. The Father, the Son, and the Holy Spirit are each fully God, each fully possessing the divine essence or nature.

The first statement is an affirmation of monotheism, a belief in the existence of only one true God, a belief that Christians share with Jews and Muslims. This affirmation, however, is affirmed together with 2 and 3, such that Christian monotheism is Trinitarian in nature, and hence distinct from Jewish and Islamic monotheism. As will be seen below, the Christian understanding of the unity of God involves a complex unity that recognizes the three persons—Father, Son, and Holy Spirit—as eternally distinct

34

persons who exist in eternal, co-equal relationships, yet without division or separation.

Statement 3 affirms the full deity of each of the three persons. The deity of the Father has never been contested in Christian history. The full deity of the Son was affirmed at the Council of Nicaea (AD 325) in response to the Arian controversy. The deity of Christ is affirmed in many ways in the biblical witness, including the following: ascription to Christ of divine titles such as "Mighty God" (Isa 9:6); "Lord" (*kurios*), when New Testament writers take Old Testament texts referring to Yahweh or Adonai and apply them to Jesus (e.g., Mark 1:2–3, citing Isa 40:3; Acts 2:21, citing Joel 2:32); ascription of divine attributes or qualities to Christ, e.g., eternity and preexistence (John 1:1; 17:5; Phil 2:5–7; Rev 22:13); not limited by space (Matt 28:20; Eph 1:22–23); universal power and authority (Matt 28:18; Eph 1:22); and self-existent life (John 1:4; 5:26).

Divine actions and prerogatives are ascribed to Christ: creation of the world (John 1:3; Col 1:16; Heb 1:2); sustaining the universe (Col 1:17); authority to forgive sins (Mark 2:5–7); object of prayer (Acts 7:59); object of worship (Matt 28:16–17; John 20:28); and final judge of all (Matt 25:31–32; John 5:22, 27). Various texts affirm the Son's equality with the Father: (John 10:29–31; 14:8–9; Phil 2:5–6; Col 2:9). Other texts ascribe the term *God* (*theos*) to Christ (John 1:1; 20:28; Titus 2:13; Heb 1:8; 2 Pet 1:1).

The full deity of the Holy Spirit was recognized and affirmed at the Council of Constantinople in 381 and incorporated into the Nicene Creed. Biblical writers ascribe omnipresence (Ps 139:7) and eternity (Heb 9:14) to the Holy Spirit. Lying to the Holy Spirit is lying to God (Acts 5:3–4). The Spirit knows fully the depths of the mind of God (1 Cor 2:10–11). To be the temple of the Holy Spirit is to be God's temple (1 Cor 3:16). The Holy Spirit is a person, with personal characteristics and actions such as teaching (Luke 12:11–12), calling and commissioning for missionary service (Acts 13:2), praying and interceding for believers (Rom 8:26), and determining the distribution of spiritual gifts (1 Cor 12:7, 11). The Holy Spirit has feelings, being grieved by sinful actions (Eph

4:30). All three statements above expressing the historic doctrine of the Trinity are thus seen to have strong biblical support.

4. The Social Trinity

One approach to the doctrine of the Trinity is known as the social Trinity. The term *social Trinity*[43] refers to a model of the Trinity in which the three persons—Father, Son, and Holy Spirit—are thought of as analogous to a family. The term *person* has had a variety of meanings in the history of theology.[44] As used here, *person* means a distinct, self-conscious subject of experiences. Father, Son, and Holy Spirit are eternally distinct (but not separated) conscious subjects within the divine nature. Each is a distinct center of mind, emotion, and will.[45] The term *person,* when applied to God, means more than when applied to humans, but it certainly does not mean less. God is the original person. Humans are images of the divine original (cf. Eph 3:14–15: "the Father, from whom all fatherhood . . . derives its name.").

As fully personal, Father, Son, and Holy Spirit each has distinct self-awareness as an *I*. At the same time each has a sense of the other as a *Thou*, and a shared consciousness as *We*. For example, in his high priestly prayer to the Father, Jesus prays that all who will believe in him may be one, "just as *you* [Father] are in me and *I* [Son, Jesus] am in you. May they also be in *us* [Father and Son, We] so that the world may believe that you have sent me" (John 17:21). This part of the prayer shows that Jesus has a consciousness of himself as *I*, and of the Father as *You* or *Thou*, and of the two of them together as *We*. This is the *I-Thou-We* consciousness of the Trinity. Just as we can toggle back and forth between several open screens or applications on our laptops, Jesus can simultaneously "toggle" back and forth between the three distinct but not separated states of consciousness, I-Thou-We. He can enter into the mind and heart of the Father without losing the sense of his own identity as an *I*, and at the same time have the consciousness of being a *We*: a unity of heart, mind, and will as Father and Son together. At the human level, this I-Thou-We unity of consciousness in a Christian marriage, friendship, or fellowship in the church is a reflection of and participation in the I-Thou-We consciousness of the Trinity.

This state of consciousness is the ideal one for joyful and fruitful worship, fellowship, and ministry in the church. This state of unity of mind was exemplified in the remarkable prayer meeting before Pentecost (Acts 1:14: "they *all joined together* constantly in prayer") and in the united reception of the Holy Spirit on the day of Pentecost itself: "All of them were filled with the Holy Spirit" (Acts 2:4). All were later filled because all were earlier of one mind. As noted earlier, the word translated as "joined together" in Acts 1:14 (*homothumadon*) literally means "of one mind," or as we might say today, "on the same page." The "one-mindedness" of those who prayed was an example of *I-Thou-We* consciousness. This state of mind—reflecting the life and mind of the Trinity—was the unity of heart and mind for which Jesus had prayed in John 17, and was the gateway to the united reception of the power of the Spirit in Acts 2:4. In short, united *I-Thou-We* consciousness in the church is the pathway to the spiritual empowerment of the church.

The personal characteristics of the Holy Spirit (thinking, willing, calling, sending, grieving) have already been noted. Further, with respect to the Son, Jesus prayed that the Father glorify him with the glory that "I had with you before the world began" (John 17:5). The words of Jesus express a distinct awareness of an *I* and a *Thou* (the Father) that was not limited to his earthly human experiences that began with the incarnation. His awareness reaches back into eternity in his preincarnate state. In the great Christ hymn of Philippians 2:6–11, the apostle Paul stated that Christ, before the incarnation, "did not consider equality with God something to be grasped, but emptied himself, taking the form of a servant" (Phil 2:6). This text indicates that in his eternal, preexistent state, the Son could reflect on his equality with the Father, and yet consciously decide to lay aside that divine glory in the incarnation.

The Holy Spirit knows the thoughts of God: "The Spirit searches all things, even the deep things of God" (1 Cor 2:11). This text reveals a distinction between the self-awareness of the Spirit and the self-awareness of God the Father. The Spirit intercedes for the saints in accordance with the Father's will, and the Father knows the mind of the Spirit (Rom 8:27). The Spirit and the Father are aware of each other as subjects, each distinct from the other. The Spirit of the Son, i.e., the Holy Spirit, cries out to the Father in the hearts of God's adopted children: "God sent the Spirit of his Son into our hearts, the Spirit who calls out, 'Abba, Father'" (Gal 4:6). This shows that the Spirit addresses the Father as a subject distinct, but not separated, from himself. Spirit and Father have reciprocal awareness of each other as distinct subjects. These texts, taken together, provide a biblical basis for understanding that distinct states of *I-Thou-We* awareness characterize not only the economic Trinity in time, but also the immanent Trinity in eternity.

These biblical texts give a basis for recognizing that Father, Son, and Holy Spirit are distinct centers of consciousness, but not separated from one another. The three undivided divine persons are one God—not three Gods—because all three share the one undivided divine nature. In the social Trinity model, Father, Son, and Holy Spirit are distinct persons, always in loving and holy relationship with one another. This model suggests analogies for healthy relationships in the family and the church: husbands, wives, friends united in holy, loving relationships, with distinct personalities and actions, but never acting independently or in separation from one another.

5. Doctrine of the Trinity: Applications for Other Christian Doctrines

Subsequent chapters will develop other implications of the doctrine of the Trinity for Christian life and ministry. Some are briefly suggested here.

Theology, the doctrine of God: God's Trinitarian nature, being fundamental to the nature of God and to the distinctive Christian understanding of God, should be studied before rather than after studying the existence and attributes of the One God.[46] To highlight the personal nature of this triune God the moral attributes (holiness, love, justice, mercy, etc.) should be discussed before the metaphysical attributes (omnipotence, omniscience, omnipresence, etc.).[47] God as the holy, loving Father of Jesus Christ, known in the Spirit, is the center of biblical revelation. The concept *perichoresis*, fundamental to the nature and persons of God, informs our understanding of the attributes of God, which co-inhere and mutually qualify one another. God's love is a holy love, and God's holiness is a loving holiness. God's love is a just love, and his justice a loving justice. His wisdom is a powerful wisdom, and his power is a wise power—and so for all the divine attributes.

Revelation: A Christian understanding of revelation reflects the Trinitarian nature of God with respect to revelation's origin, purpose, process, and reception. All of God's self-disclosure to humans originates in the joint actions of the triune God: from the Father, through the Son, by the Spirit. Reception of and response to revelation is by the Spirit, through the Son, and to the Father.

Revelation, by act or words, reflects communication that has existed eternally between the persons of the Godhead. The Father and the Son speak to each other in fellowship with the Holy Spirit. The fundamental purpose of God's revelation is to bring us into fellowship with himself, so we come to share the life of the Trinity: "they in us" (John 17:21).[48]

Creation: Creation, providence, and redemption are joint actions of all three persons of the Trinity. Creation proceeds from the Father, is enacted by the Son, and perfected by the Spirit. Creation, originating in the powerful and gracious will of the Father, has the curse upon it removed in Christ (cf. Col 1:20), and is glorified by the Spirit, so that creation can enjoy the glorious freedom of the children of God (Rom 8:21–23).

Anthropology and *Soteriology:* Humanity and redemption. Human beings, made in the image of God, are redeemed for the purpose of enjoying fellowship with the Trinity (Eph 1:3, 4; John 17:21). Our fundamental purpose is grounded in the Trinity. "The chief end of man is to glorify God and to enjoy him forever."[49] Salvation, which is from the Father, through the Son, in the Spirit (1 Pet 1:2) is the fulfillment of humanity's highest purpose.

Ecclesiology: doctrine of the church. The church, the redeemed people of God, reflects the triune nature of God in both its being and actions. The church is the family of God the Father, the body and bride of Christ the Son, and the temple of the Holy Spirit. The church's worship is a participation in the Son's praise of the Father in the Spirit (Luke 10:21; Heb 2:5).[50] Discipleship and mission are done not by human individuals alone, but in partnership with the Trinity (Matt 28:19, 20; John 8:28, 29; 15:5; 1 Pet 4:11).[51] Christian partnership in ministry reflects the partnership of Father, Son, and Holy Spirit in the acts of creation, providence, and redemption.[52]

Ethics: Biblical ethical standards reflect the life, mind, and internal relationships of the Trinity. Being like-minded (Phil 2:2) and preferring others in honor (Phil 2:3) reflects the Son's relationship to the Father (Phil 2:5–7). The apostle Paul's exhortation for Christian self-emptying follows from Christ's self-emptying, his taking the form of a servant. The Christian life should not reflect the mindset Me, Myself, and I. Instead, the Christian life should reflect the mindset I-Thou-We, reflecting the way Father, Son, and Spirit honor one another. This mindset minimizes conflicts in the church and maximizes the unity for which Christ prayed (John 17:21).

Eschatology: the doctrine of the last things. Eschatology includes the return of Christ, the general resurrection, and the last judgment. More broadly, it points to the completion of God's purposes in creation, providence, and redemption. Creation will be freed from the curse and filled with the glory of God (Rev 21:11; 22:1–3). The creation will be reconciled under the headship of Christ the Son (Col 1:20; Eph 1:10). God's people will be brought into perfect communion with the triune God and the body of Christ (John 17:21; Eph 3:19). God's people will enjoy in fullness the love, joy, and peace shared by Father, Son, and Spirit. God will be all in all (Eph 1:23; 1 Cor 15:28).

Union with Christ, Glory in the Spirit:
Seraphim of Sarov

Seraphim of Sarov, an eighteenth-century hermit in the forests of Russia, is one of the most famous holy men in the Russian Orthodox tradition. Recognized as a saint, he was renowned for his practice of the presence of God and personal holiness. The following account relates a conversation between Seraphim and Motovilov, a younger admirer and follower of the saint:

> Motovilov asked, "How can I know if the Holy Spirit is with me or not?" Seraphim gave him examples from the lives of the saints and apostles, and then took him by the shoulder and said to him, "We are both now in the Spirit." It was as though Motovilov's spiritual eyes had been opened, for he saw that the saint's face was shining like the sun. In his heart Motovilov felt a sense of joy and peace, and a sense of warmth as if it were summer. Seraphim said to him, "Do not fear . . . you would not even be able to see me if you yourself were not in the fullness of the Spirit. Thank the Lord for his mercy toward us." Then Motovilov understood what the descent of the Holy Spirit and his transfiguration of a person meant.[53]

This remarkable account recalls the statement of the apostle Paul in 2 Corinthians 3:18: "And we all, who contemplate the Lord's glory, are being transformed into his likeness with ever increasing glory, which comes from the Lord, who is Spirit."

Union with Christ: Who Am I?
How Should I Do Ministry?

This section examines a crucial biblical teaching for Christian living: union with Christ.[54] The Holy Spirit connects us in a living relationship to a living Christ—not in an outward connection to a human organization.

Vine, body, and bride are living familiar biblical metaphors for our union with Christ. Jesus is the true vine; we are the branches (John 15:1–8). We are organically connected to Christ; all fruitfulness flows from him. Without remaining in him, we produce no lasting spiritual fruit. This image of the vine and branches is Trinitarian: the Son is the vine, the Father the vine dresser (John 15:1), and, implicitly, the Holy Spirit is the life-giving water that flows into the vine and into the branches.

The images of body and bride are developed by the apostle Paul. We are living members of the body of Christ, a living body of which Christ is the head (Rom 12; 1 Cor 12; Eph 4). The body functions in a healthy manner when all are subject to the head and to one another, and when each member functions in the power of the Spirit. Paul also teaches that the church is the bride of Christ (Eph 5:22–33), his beloved for whom he gave his life. All three images—vine, body, bride—are organic, not mechanical. These images show that our relationship to Christ is not primarily one of institutional membership but rather one of intimate relationship.

In the Pauline and Johannine texts, union with Christ is expressed with the prepositions *in* and *with*. We are *in Christ* and Christ is *in us*. We are *with Christ*, and Christ is *with us*. We were chosen *in Christ* before the world was created (Eph 1:4). This union with Christ was taught by Christ before his cross and resurrection (John 14:20, 23; 15:5; 17:22–23, 26). Union with Christ is effected by the Holy Spirit at conversion. We died with Christ (Rom 6:3). We were baptized into the body of Christ (1 Cor 12:13). We were raised with Christ (Eph 2:6).

But what does being *in Christ* mean? Should we have a conscious awareness of union with Christ, at least occasionally? Or is union with Christ just a metaphor or figure of speech—not a conscious experience?

In his farewell discourse Jesus promised, "On that day you will realize that I am in my Father, and that you are in me, and I am in you" (John 14:20). Jesus spoke of the sending of the Holy Spirit: "I will ask the Father, and he will give you another Counselor . . . You know him for he lives with you and will be in you"

(John 14:16–17). Jesus expected that his disciples would have a conscious awareness of their reception of the Holy Spirit. Just as Jesus and the Father shared their inner lives, so Jesus, through the Spirit, shares his inner life with us.

In close human friendships we say that we "let our hair down." Sometimes we let friends see the "real me." We are saying, "I am letting you into my life; let me into yours." As human beings we are "hard-wired for empathy," as neuroscience tells us. We have a capacity to feel the feelings of others, to share their subjectivity. The Holy Spirit is God himself, connecting our subjectivity with his own, pouring the Father's love for Jesus into our own hearts. "God has poured out his love into our hearts by the Holy Spirit, whom he has given us" (Rom 5:5). Being in Christ means that we can experience the love, joy, and peace that Jesus experiences with the Father as he shares his experience with us (John 17:13, 26, 27).

There are barriers to experiencing union with Christ. One is a misunderstanding of the nature and value of biblical metaphors or metaphors in general. Metaphors such as the vine and branches (John 15:1–8) at times may be dismissed as "just figures of speech," as literary ornaments that contribute nothing to essential meaning, better replaced with more literal statements. This way of thinking about metaphor reflects the Enlightenment and modern scientific valuing of the literal and mathematical over the poetic, metaphorical, and symbolic. From this perspective, literal statements are truer than nonliteral ones. Poetry and metaphor may evoke emotions, but do not add to understanding. Metaphorical statements should be reduced to literal ones.

Recent studies in cognitive science, linguistics, and philosophy, however, demonstrate that metaphor is fundamental to our knowledge of the world. Metaphors are linked to our bodies and brains, connecting us to the objects in the world around us.[55] Metaphor connects bodily experience—grasping a tool with our hands—to intellectual and emotional experience—grasping an idea with our minds. Metaphor gives us richer experiences and connections to the world than do literal expressions such as mathematical formulas. Metaphorical thinking is essential, not incidental, both in common sense and in biblical theology.

Our union with Christ expressed in the metaphor of vine and branches is not "just a figure of speech" that should be reduced to a more literal statement such as, "To bear fruit, continually think about Christ and obey his commands." Such literal interpretations of the metaphor, while true, miss the deeper significance of the language. Union with Christ, like the union of vine and branches, is not just an idea in the mind, but a metaphysical reality: a living, spiritual relationship that is true even when we are not thinking about it. We are truly connected and united to Christ by the Holy Spirit, not only when we are thinking about Christ, but even when we are asleep. Similarly, we are still married, in a continuously existing marriage relationship, even when we are not thinking the thought "I am married." A relationship such as union with Christ or marriage is not just a wispy idea flitting about in our minds, but a reality shaping our lives.

Biblical metaphors do not take us further away from biblical truth, but deeper into the truth to which they refer. Images of material and visible things—vines and branches—do not merely evoke ideas in our minds, but, through the presence and actions of the Holy Spirit, connect us experientially to the spiritual and invisible realities to which they point: to Christ and to the Father who pour their love into our hearts (Rom 5:5).

Biblical metaphors are not *bare* symbols but *effective* symbols. The symbol H_2O written on a whiteboard by the chemistry professor is a bare symbol: it points to a reality that is absent. H_2O does not convey the reality to which it points. I cannot drink the symbol H_2O on the whiteboard. *Vine and branch*, however, can, through faith and the Spirit, become an effective symbol that makes present and conveys to me the reality to which it refers. As we meditate by faith, in the Spirit, on a text such as John 15:1–8, the vine and the branches, we can experience and enjoy our union with Christ as he imparts his life to us through his word and Spirit.

Another barrier to grasping the concept of union with Christ is misunderstanding the Pauline and Johannine terms expressing this union: we are *in* Christ and Christ is *in* us; both use the preposition *in* (*'en*). Does the word *in* mean "contained within" in some physical or spatial sense, like coffee contained in my coffee cup? Am I literally inside Christ and is Christ literally inside me? Is this what union with Christ means?

This use of *in* means, however, that I am in Christ and that Christ is in me in a spiritual and relational sense, rather than in a literal and physical sense. Christ and I both have physical bodies, but Christ and I are not only physical bodies. Human beings—including Jesus, now in heaven—are *extended selves*—not circumscribed selves. We are selves centered in physical bodies, but not selves whose presence and actions are limited to the physical boundaries of our bodies.[56] Christ has a mind and a will that extend and impart his thoughts and feelings into me. As a human being, I too have a mind and a will that can extend and impart my thoughts and feelings to other people—including to Christ— by speaking to them through various means, such as face to face or electronically. In so doing we get "into" the other person. The Holy Spirit, through the words of Jesus, imparts Christ's heart and mind into our hearts and minds—he comes, relationally and spiritually, into us. In our prayers, the Holy Spirit takes the words of our hearts and brings them into the heart and mind of Christ—we enter, relationally and spiritually, into him. This is how Christ is *in* us and how we are *in* Christ.

Because we are united to Christ, we are in the presence of Christ even on occasions when we may not be expecting to experience his presence. For example, Jesus opened the Scriptures to the disciples on the road to Emmaus—while they stood in his presence, not yet recognizing him: "And beginning with Moses and all the Prophets, he explained to them what was said in all the Scriptures concerning himself" (Luke 24:27). In the Spirit, and through our union with Christ, our reading Scripture can become our own Emmaus road experience. Our union with Christ is the basis for those "Aha" moments when the Holy Spirit illuminates the biblical text, making it come alive for us. Christ and the Holy Spirit can cause us to say, as did the disciples at Emmaus, "Were not our hearts burning within us while he [Christ] . . . opened the Scriptures to us?" (Luke 24:32). The disciples were experiencing a Bible study in the presence of Christ, illuminated by the Holy Spirit. That, too, can be the believer's experience today.

God inspired Scripture to benefit not only the original readers, but also all believers until the end of time. We are meant to see ourselves in the biblical stories, since God had us in mind when giving the Bible to the church. "These things happened to them as examples and were written down . . . for us, on whom the fulfillment of the ages has come" (1 Cor 10:11). Paul taught the Corinthian church that the Old Testament narratives of Israel's years in the wilderness—including their idolatry and disobedience—were recorded also for the instruction of the New Testament church. God intended the new Israel in the new covenant to see itself in the stories of old Israel recorded in the old covenant Scriptures.

Consider the following story. Two friends, Carlos and Philippe, were watching TV in Carlos's home in California's Central Valley. The show, a docudrama called *The Mexican-American Experience*, featured the story of Caesar Chavez and the United Farm Workers' struggle for better wages and conditions for farm workers in the Central Valley. Carlos's French-Canadian college friend, Philippe, was visiting from Montreal. Philippe watched the documentary with interest, but he viewed it as an outsider. This was not his personal story. Carlos, however, watched it through different eyes. Carlos and his family had been undocumented Mexicans who crossed the border to pick produce in the Central Valley, later becoming citizens. "Look, that's me with Caesar Chavez!" exclaimed Carlos, pointing to the screen. "I'm in this story." Indeed, just as Carlos was an extra in the docudrama starring Caesar Chavez, as believers we have become actors in the real-life biblical story starring Jesus Christ, directed by God the Father, and written by the Holy Spirit.

There is even more to the story. Also watching with them were Roberto Diaz, who played Chavez, Maria Santiago, the screen writer, and Grayson Carter, the director. Before watching the documentary, Carlos introduced Roberto, Maria, and Grayson to

Philippe and said, "I would like you to meet Roberto, who played Chavez, and Maria, who wrote the script, and Grayson, who was the director. I met them when I was an extra in the film, and we later became friends."

Consider the baptism of Jesus in light of biblical statements about our spiritual position in Christ. God chose us in Christ before the creation of the world (Eph 1:4). God raised us up with Christ and seated us with him in the heavenly places (Eph 2:6). As we meditate on Matthew's account (Matt 3:13–17), we read as those who are united by the Spirit to Christ in the heavenly places. Our spirit is connected to his spirit by the Holy Spirit. "He who unites himself with the Lord is one with him in Spirit" (1 Cor 6:17). We are meditating on the text in the presence of Christ, who is the central figure in this story and in Scripture as a whole (John 5:39). In light of Ephesians 1:4 we realize that God the Father from all eternity viewed us as in Christ—connected to Christ and to the events in the life of Christ, including his baptism. We were written into the story of Christ from the beginning. Our stories are taken up into Christ's. In God's foreknowledge, he saw us as beneficiaries of all the saving acts of his Son.

Christ accepted baptism from John not because he needed to confess his own sins—he had none to confess. He accepted baptism for us, voluntarily identifying himself with all the people of God, past, present, and future. His baptism anticipates his substitutionary atonement for the sins of his people. In our union with Christ we participate in his baptism, his death, his resurrection, and his experience with Pentecost. We were written in the script from eternity.

Jesus' baptism is a picture not only of Jesus' experience, but also of ours in Christ. In a spiritual or mystical sense, we were with Jesus as he stood in the Jordan River being baptized, not for his sins, but for ours. In God's plan, Jesus' baptism was preordained to be an illustration of our own baptism and reception of the Holy Spirit. The Father's words to Jesus are also meant for us: "You are my beloved son; with you I am well pleased."[57] We read the text in the living presence of the Father, the producer-director who had us in mind from the beginning. We read it in the presence of the Spirit, the screenwriter who wrote the script and explains it to us. We read it in the presence of the Son, the star of the show, who called us to be not just an extra in the drama, but close personal friends. "I no longer call you servants, because a servant does not know his master's business. Instead, I have called you friends, for everything that I have learned from my Father I have made known to you" (John 15:15). We meditate upon the text not as outsiders or disinterested parties, but as insiders who were meant to see themselves in the biblical story and as beneficiaries of Jesus' work.

Union with Christ has important implications for the practice of ministry. In union with Christ, we can serve the way Jesus served: not merely in human energy, but in the ordinary and extraordinary energy of the Spirit. Jesus promised, "Anyone who has faith in me will do what I have been doing. He will do even greater things than these, because I am going to the Father" (John 14:12). Peter did "greater things" than Jesus, not that his miracles or message were inherently greater, but they were greater in geographic reach and numbers converted. Three thousand were converted through Peter's Pentecost sermon (Acts 2:41), a greater converting response to Peter's sermon than any single sermon of Jesus recorded in the Gospels. Jesus preached before the outpouring of the Spirit at Pentecost; Peter preached after. What a difference the Holy Spirit made! Peter had his eyes fixed on the exalted Lord Jesus in heaven. Being filled with the Spirit and in union with Christ, he proclaimed Jesus as the exalted Lord and Messiah: "The Lord said to my Lord: 'Sit at my right hand until I make your enemies a footstool for your feet'" (Acts 2:35 = Ps 110:1).

Our Christian service can be empowered this way as well: eyes fixed on Jesus, serving in union with Christ, filled with the Spirit. Peter's preaching was remarkably effective not because of his human homiletical ability but rather because Christ poured his Spirit out on Peter. The Holy Spirit caused Peter to remember Scriptures he had learned earlier (Joel 2, Ps 16; 110). The Holy Spirit then illuminated them to produce conviction of sin in those who heard. Peter's listeners were cut to the heart (Acts 2:37). Jesus'

48

promise of the convicting work of the Spirit was being fulfilled: "When he [the Counselor, the Spirit] comes, he will convict the world of guilt" (John 16:8). Ordinary supernatural actions of the Spirit—illumination of Scriptures, conviction of sin, repentance— produced extraordinary supernatural results: through a single sermon, 3,000 conversions.

Leading a person to salvation in Christ is a blessing greater than miraculous healing. Healing is a great blessing—but temporary—because the person healed will eventually die. Leading a person to salvation, however, is a greater blessing that lasts forever.

What does it mean to do ministry the way Jesus did it? John's Gospel gives us answers. At Jerusalem's Bethesda pool Jesus healed a man who had been an invalid for thirty-eight years (John 5:1–15). He was only one of many at the pool who needed healing. Why did Jesus heal only one? We have Jesus' answer: "The Son can do nothing by himself; he can only do what he sees the Father doing, because whatever the Father does the Son also does" (John 5:19). Jesus never acted independently. Evidently, it was the Father's will to heal only that specific paralytic on that occasion. He discerned what the Father was doing in a situation and then joined in the Father's work. Jesus practiced ministry in the presence of God and in partnership with God.

In teaching and preaching Jesus first listened to God before he spoke about God:[58] "I do nothing on my own but speak just what the Father has taught me. The one who sent me is with me; he has not left me alone, for I always do what pleases him" (John 8:28b, 29). Jesus knew that the Father was the unseen third party, present in every encounter he had with a needy person. He prayerfully listened for the Father's voice before speaking to that person.

When we act independently from God, on our own human power, we produce no lasting fruit. Acting independently from God is the root of all sin. When we remain in Christ, we produce much lasting fruit (John 15:5, 16). How do we remain in Christ? We remain in Christ the same way Christ remained in the Father: remembering our dependence on God, listening to God before speaking,[59] sensing what God is doing, then joining God in doing it—as Jesus did at the pool of Bethesda.

When having a serious conversation with someone, to be most helpful, we can say a brief silent prayer: "Jesus, be with me now, help me to listen deeply, and to sense what is really going on." We are inviting Jesus into the conversation as an unseen third party who can impart the needed wisdom. We listen prayerfully, depending on the Holy Spirit to give us the right words to say.

Acting in partnership with Christ in ministry can protect us from burning out in ministry. We recognize that Christ is the primary agent; we are secondary agents. In the last analysis, only he can finish the work of God. He is the musician; we are the instruments in his hands. He produces the fruit; we are the branches through which he produces fruit. I tell theology students, "I can't really teach you any theology. Only God can give you a heart knowledge of himself. I am just his teaching assistant. Listen to him." Jesus is the real pastor of the church. We are his assistant pastors, working in partnership with the master, following the one who has promised to be with us to the end of the age (Matt 28:20).

Realized Eschatology: Arrival of the Spirit; the End of Cessationism

---

William Haslam, A Life Changed by the Holy Spirit

John Stott recounts the remarkable change in the life of William Haslam:

> William Haslam was a Church of England clergyman who was ordained in 1842, serving a parish in Cornwall, but who felt spiritually dry inside. In 1851, nine years after his ordination, while preaching on the gospel text for that Sunday, "What think ye of Christ?," the Holy Spirit opened his eyes to truly see the Christ of whom

he was speaking, and opened his heart to believe in him. The change that came over Haslam was so obvious that a visiting preacher who was in the church that day jumped up and shouted, "The preacher has been converted! Hallelujah!'"

His voice was joined spontaneously by 300 or 400 of those who were present in the congregation. The news spread like wildfire in the region, that "the preacher had been converted, and that by his own sermon, in his own pulpit." Haslam's conversion was the beginning of a great renewal in the parish, which lasted for almost three years, with conversions almost daily, and a vivid sense of the presence of God.[60]

This third section focuses on the powerful New Testament truth, realized eschatology—the return and arrival of the Spirit.[61] In the Judaism of Jesus' day, the rabbis saw a timeline of history divided into *this age* and the *age to come*. This age was dominated by evil, oppression, and bondage. In the age to come, the Messiah would bring Israel's freedom from Roman oppression, the observance of the Sabbath and of the law of Moses, the return of the Spirit and the living voice of prophecy.

The New Testament writers realized that the age to come and the kingdom of God had already begun to arrive in Jesus' life, death, resurrection, and the outpouring of the Holy Spirit. The kingdom, however, would not be fully realized until the return of Jesus at the end of history. The early church lived in the tension of a time in which the old order of this age overlapped with the new order of the age to come.

This sense that the age to come had begun is reflected in Hebrews 6:5, where the writer stated that his readers "have tasted the goodness of the word of God, and the powers of the coming age." Those who heard the voice of Jesus and believed his message of eternal life had already, in the Spirit, experienced the resurrection that would occur bodily in the future (John 5:25). In their conversion believers already were raised spiritually with Jesus and already were seated with him in the heavenly places (Eph 2:6). They already were justified: "Therefore, since we have been justified by faith, we have peace with God through our Lord Jesus Christ" (Rom 5:1). They already were adopted: "Because you are sons, God sent the Spirit of his Son into our hearts" (Gal 4:6). They already were sanctified: "By one sacrifice he has made perfect forever those who are being sanctified" (Heb 10:14). All three—justification, adoption, and sanctification—will be fully realized when Christ returns.

A pivotal aspect of realized eschatology is the return of the Spirit predicted by the prophets, ending the long intertestamental period of cessation of the Spirit's activity. The long-awaited return of the Spirit is foreshadowed in Luke's infancy narratives. The Spirit is at work in John the Baptist from birth (Luke 1:15), in the conception of Jesus (Luke 1:35), in the inspired utterances of Elizabeth and Mary (Luke 1:41–55), in the song of Zechariah (Luke 1:67–79), and in the responses of Simeon and Anna (Luke 2:25–38). The preaching of John the Baptist in the Judean wilderness was the sign of the return of the Spirit to Israel and of the renewal of prophecy—God's living voice.

Jesus promised the gift and power of the Spirit: "You will receive power when the Holy Spirit comes on you" (Acts 1:8). Jesus' promise was fulfilled on the day of Pentecost, when they were all filled with the Holy Spirit (Acts 2:4). The Spirit's arrival fulfilled not only familiar Old Testament texts such as Joel 2:28–32, but many others as well. God would return in the Spirit to dwell with his people:

> "You will not let your Holy One see decay. . . . You will fill me with joy in your presence, with eternal pleasures at your right hand." (Ps 16:10, 11; Acts 2:27, 28)

> "Then the LORD will create over all of Mount Zion and over those who assemble there a cloud of smoke by day and a glow of flaming fire by night; over all the glory will be a canopy." (Isa 4:5)

"I will pour out my Spirit on your offspring, and my blessing on your descendants." (Isa 44:3)

"I will give you a new heart and put a new spirit in you . . . I will put my Spirit in you and move you to follow my decrees and be careful to keep my laws. . . . You will be my people, and I will be your God." (Ezek 36:26–28)

"I will put breath in you, and you will come to life. Then you will know that I am the LORD. . . . I will put my Spirit in you and you will live . . . You will know that I the LORD have spoken." (Ezek 37:6, 14)

"I will no longer hide my face from them, for I will pour out my Spirit on the house of Israel." (Ezek 39:29)

"The desired of all nations will come, and I will fill this house with glory." (Hag 2:7)

"Jerusalem will be a city without walls . . . I myself will be a wall of fire around it . . . and I will be its glory within . . . Shout and be glad, O Daughter of Zion. For I am coming, and will live among you." (Zech 2:4–5, 10)

"I will return to Zion and dwell in Jerusalem. . . . The mountain of the LORD Almighty will be called the Holy Mountain." (Zech 8:3)

The return of the Holy Spirit was an integral part of the good news announced by Jesus. God was fulfilling what he had promised long before in the prophets. He was pouring out his Spirit on all God's people—not only on prophets, priests, and kings as in former days. The full arrival and availability of the Holy Spirit for all Christians, for all churches, for the entire church age—realized eschatology—means that all God's people can expect to see spiritual fruit and changed lives.

The Holy Spirit acts at three different levels in our Christian service: the natural, the ordinary supernatural, and the extraordinary supernatural (miraculous). The Holy Spirit, who is the Lord and Giver of life, is the creator of all natural abilities. As the apostle

Paul reminded the Corinthians, "What do you have that you did not receive? And if you did receive it, why do you boast as though you did not?" (1 Cor 4:7). "In him we live and move and have our being" (Acts 17:28). Ministry in natural energy depends on natural human ability and effort. Ministry in the natural produces natural results.

The ordinary supernatural, the middle level of action, is often overlooked. Natural abilities are not abandoned but enhanced and energized by the Spirit. The ordinary supernatural is the quiet and undramatic action of the Spirit, changing lives and the fruit of the Spirit. The supernatural power of God is not only present at the third, extraordinary level. *Supernatural* does not always mean spectacular signs, wonders, and miracles. In the long run, the quieter actions of the Holy Spirit are more important than dramatic miracles. Preaching in the ordinary supernatural is anointed preaching, producing conviction of sin and lasting fruit in the hearers' lives. On the day of Pentecost, Peter used his natural abilities—his human voice and his knowledge of Scripture—but his natural ability was elevated by the supernatural anointing of the Holy Spirit to produce remarkable conversions.

In Acts 2, the day of Pentecost, we see examples of all three levels of the Spirit's action: the natural (Peter's human voice and ability); the extraordinary supernatural (speaking in tongues and flames of fire); and the ordinary supernatural (conviction of sin, repentance, and conversion). Extraordinary manifestations of the Spirit such as flames of fire may be temporary. The conversions produced by the ordinary supernatural action of the Spirit were lasting. God may sovereignly choose to witness to the truth of the gospel by performing signs and wonders (extraordinary supernatural), but miracles are not under human control. In all our Christian service we should pray that the Holy Spirit will elevate our natural abilities, preparation, and hard work up into the level of the ordinary supernatural and produce the fruit of the Spirit and changed lives.

Wesley at Aldersgate:
The Ordinary Supernatural Work of the Spirit

In May 1738, John Wesley attended a meeting of Moravians at Aldersgate in London. He heard someone reading the preface of Luther's commentary on Romans. In his journal, he described his experience:

> About a quarter before nine, while he was describing the change which God works in the heart through faith in Christ, I felt my heart strangely warmed. I felt I did trust in Christ, in Christ alone, for salvation; and an assurance was given me, that He had taken away my sins, even mine, and saved me from the law of sin and death.[62]

The Holy Spirit powerfully illuminated the truth of justification by faith alone in Christ alone, making it real in Wesley's heart, as well as in his mind. He knew that his life had been changed. This encounter with the renewing work of the Holy Spirit was a turning point in Wesley's life. The ordinary supernatural action of the Spirit, illuminating and applying the truth of the gospel, changed John Wesley's life forever.

The Danger of Ministry Done Only in the Natural

Western churches are tempted to operate in a natural mode because we have so many natural resources: money, buildings, programs, education, credentials, medicine, technology. Friedrich Schleiermacher, the nineteenth-century father of modern liberal theology, made a telling observation about the German churches of his day:

> Even if it cannot be strictly proved that the Church's power of working miracles has died out . . . yet in general it is undeniable that, in view of the *great advantage in power and civilization which the Christian peoples possess*

55

over the non-Christian, almost without exception, the preachers of today do not need such signs.[63]

Schleiermacher, reacting to Roman Catholic claims of miraculous powers, said, in effect, that ministers of his time did not need supernatural help to do ministry and missions. The human resources of technology and Western civilization were sufficient. Could Schleiermacher's observation about the liberal churches of his day be true of evangelical churches of our day?

This danger faced the early church as well. The apostle Paul was concerned that the churches in Galatia, after "beginning with the Spirit," were now in danger of trying to attain their goal merely "by human effort" (Gal 3:3). The Galatians began with the supernatural power of the Spirit but were in danger of continuing in the Christian life with only the power of the natural. Jesus, in contrast, both began and continued in the power of the Spirit: Jesus, after receiving the Holy Spirit at his baptism (Luke 3:21) and being led by the Spirit in the wilderness (Luke 4:1), returned to Galilee in the power of the Spirit (Luke 4:14). The apostle Peter stated that Jesus' entire ministry continued in the power of the Spirit: "God anointed Jesus of Nazareth with the Holy Spirit and power, and . . . he went around doing good and healing all who were under the power of the devil, because God was with him" (Acts 10:38).

Having begun our Christian lives through the work of the Spirit in our conversion, we must continue our Christian service with a consciousness of our continuing dependence on the Spirit. We must continually remind ourselves that Christ is the vine; we are only branches, and that apart from him we cannot produce lasting fruit. Our natural human actions can help people to a certain extent, by mitigating their ignorance or suffering, but only Christ, through the Spirit, can produce changes in people that will last eternally. The fruit of the Spirit can only be produced by the Holy Spirit, not by our human energy. Human agency is instrumental, but not in itself sufficient. "I [Paul] planted the seed, Apollos watered, but God made it grow" (1 Cor 3:6).

Prayer is the normal means by which we put ourselves in touch with the ordinary and extraordinary power of the Spirit.

Jesus, at his baptism, received the Spirit as he was praying (Luke 3:21). Before being filled with the Spirit on the day of Pentecost the early believers united in corporate prayer (Acts 1:14). After being released from arrest by the Sanhedrin, Peter and John returned to the gathered believers and prayed. After praying, "they were filled with the Holy Spirit and spoke the word of God boldly" (Acts 4:31). At his baptism, Jesus, through prayer, aligned his mind and will with the Father's, and then received the Spirit. The early believers, following this pattern, through prayer, aligned their minds and wills with Christ's, and received fresh empowerment by the Spirit. This spiritual alignment through prayer allows the Spirit to flow from the Father to the Son, and from the Son into us and the body of Christ. Only the Holy Spirit—invoked in prayer, before, during, and after ministry—can make the seeds of Scripture grow in the hearts of those who hear it.

The full arrival of the Spirit in the new covenant makes the beatific vision—glimpsing Christ in his glory—not merely a distant hope in the future, reserved for great saints and mystics, but a possibility for Christian believers now. For much of church history the common belief has been that believers will see Christ's glory only when they die or when Christ returns. Jesus prayed that his followers would be with him where he was and see his glory (John 17:24). Will Jesus' prayer be answered only when we die?

Paul offered a different answer: "And we *all*, who with unveiled faces contemplate the Lord's glory, are being transformed into his image with ever-increasing glory, which comes from the Lord, who is the Spirit" (2 Cor 3:18, emphasis added). Paul described an experience—beholding the Lord's glory and being transformed by it—that was being experienced by the Corinthians in the present, not just reserved for them in the future. This experience was not just for himself as an apostle, or for great mystics, but for all believers. Moses saw the glory of God on Mount Sinai and came down from the mountain with a glowing face (Exod 34:29). Paul taught that Christians, by faith and in the Spirit, can behold the glory of the risen Christ during worship, meditation, and prayer—and be changed by it. Through meditation on the Scriptures in faith we may catch glimpses of the risen Lord's glory through spiritual eyes. Paul prayed that the eyes of our hearts would be enlightened (Eph 1:18). Believers will see Christ's glory fully when he returns and we appear with him in glory (Col 3:4).

Finally, realized eschatology means that new covenant believers have been given spiritual gifts for ministry (Rom 12; 1 Cor 12, 14; Eph 4).[64] Christians can know that they have received one or more such spiritual gifts. Pastors and teachers need to teach these truths, so that church members can identify and use their gifts to build up the body of Christ. A church where members know and use their spiritual gifts is a healthy, flourishing church. This is normal Christianity: life in the Spirit (Rom 8:1–17).

Questions for Discussion

1. Do you think that the doctrine of the Trinity is poorly understood and neglected in many churches today? What do you think are the factors that have contributed to this neglect? Do you think that the Trinity should be a model for Christian life and ministry? Can you give some examples of how such a model could be applied in your teaching and preaching?

2. Do you agree with the statement, "Union with Christ is very central in the theologies of Paul and John"? What illustrations or analogies would you use to teach and preach this truth? How would you try to show people in your church or youth group that this concept is really important for their relationship to God and to Christian service?

3. Explain the concept *realized eschatology*. Can you connect realized eschatology to the distinctions between the natural, the ordinary supernatural, and the extraordinary supernatural? What difference should realized eschatology make in the way that we do ministry in the church? Can you give specific examples?

For Further Reading

Donald Fairbairn, *Life in the Trinity: An Introduction to Theology with the Help of the Fathers.*

Rich insights from the church fathers and practical application for life and ministry.

James B. Torrance, *Worship, Community and the Triune God of Grace.*

Worship and community in the church, rooted in the Trinity.

Gordon D. Fee, *God's Empowering Presence: The Holy Spirit in the Letters of Paul.*

Excellent exposition of Paul's teachings on the presence and power of the Spirit.

3

THREE CRUCIAL PRACTICES FOR SPIRITUAL RENEWAL

Worship, Meditation, Ministry

Practicing God's Presence
in Worship, Meditation, and Discipleship

CHAPTERS TWO AND THREE considered three biblical texts and three biblical teachings foundational for spiritual growth and church renewal: Acts 2, Matthew 28, and John 17; and the Trinity, union with Christ, and the arrival of the Spirit. These texts and doctrines point to a vitally important theme in Scripture: the life-changing presence of God with his people. The conscious awareness of God's presence enhances our enjoyment of worship, personal devotion, and discipleship.

Meeting God at the Altar: Thomas Aquinas

Thomas Aquinas was one of the greatest theologians of all time. His *Summa Theologica*, a masterwork of the high Middle Ages,

60

is one of the greatest works of Christian doctrine. Thomas's massive learning, systematic mind, and enormous energy made him a prodigiously productive Christian theologian, teacher, and writer.

On December 6, 1273, near the end of his life, Thomas was celebrating mass at Naples's St. Nicholas Chapel. While at the altar, he had a life-changing experience, causing him to give up all his dictation and writing thereafter. He left the final sections of the *Summa* unfinished. Asked why he had stopped his work, he replied cryptically, "I can write no more. All that I have written seems like straw."[1] Thomas evidently experienced a transformative encounter with God and the risen Christ—raising his previous knowledge of God to an entirely new level.

Finding God's Presence in Worship[65]

1. The Divine Presence in Biblical Revelation

God's presence—a presence that can be consciously felt—is a central biblical theme from Genesis to Revelation. God walked in the garden of Eden, the home of the human race's first parents (Gen 3:8). Because of their disobedience, Adam and Eve were banished from the garden, driven from God's presence (Gen 3:23). Cain, the first murderer, was anguished by his awareness of being "hidden from your presence" (Gen 4:14).

After the fall, God's felt presence was not entirely absent from the earth. Godly antediluvians Enoch (Gen 5:24) and Noah (Gen 6:9) "walked with God," indicating their awareness of God's presence with them.

God's presence continued with the patriarchs Abraham, Isaac, and Jacob. God appeared to Abraham, commanding him, "I am God Almighty; walk before me and be blameless" (Gen 17:1). During a period of famine God assured Isaac, "I will be with you and will bless you," and repeated this promise, appearing to Isaac in a night vision at Beersheba: "Do not be afraid, for I am with

---

1. Graves, "Article #29,"

you" (Gen 26:3, 24). In a dream at Bethel, God appeared to Jacob and assured him, "I am with you and will watch over you wherever you go," during all his sojournings (Gen 28:15). As an old man having to leave the promised land because of famine, Jacob heard God's promise in a night vision, "I will go down to Egypt with you, and I will surely bring you back again" (Gen 46:4).

Encountering God in Worship: The Story of John Park

John Park was born and raised in Korea by a mother who was indifferent to religion and a father who was an atheist. John moved to the United States, where he met his wife and enrolled in a master's degree program in film studies. When his wife was pregnant with their first child, John visited a church in Georgia. In prayer he promised God that he would serve God in the second half of his life if God supplied the financial help he needed for his education and childbirth expenses. To his amazement, he received a phone call from the hospital informing him that a local millionaire had left a large sum of money to help international students who could not afford healthcare. But even after this remarkable turn of events, John's faith did not grow.

An elder in a local church told John to pray nightly, "Holy Spirit, come." He did this for six months. One night John sat in the church auditorium listening to the choir prepare for Easter. They sang a song based on Isaiah 53. John was struck by the words. He suddenly found himself gripped by a vivid vision of the crucifixion; he said he felt the tangible presence of God's love and the depth of his own sinfulness. From that time onward John's life was changed. He read his Bible through six times each year for the next five years. Three years after his dramatic encounter with God, he decided to honor his earlier promise to God, and enrolled at Gordon-Conwell Theological Seminary to prepare for a new vocation of serving God in ministry.

The life of Moses and the events of the exodus demonstrate not only that God was present with his people but also that God's people were consciously aware of his presence. God was not passively, but actively present, blessing and saving his people. This conscious awareness of God's presence was intended to be a distinctive mark of their identity as God's special people. The presence of God was not just a thought flitting in their heads; it was a felt experience. When the LORD spoke to Moses from within the burning bush, Moses was consciously aware of God's presence: he heard God's voice. As Moses stood on this holy ground and the LORD called him to lead the people out of Egypt, Moses was, so to speak, six feet away from the living God. God was present and God was doing something: he drafted Moses for a very big job. In the exodus from Egypt, the LORD revealed his presence in the fiery pillar and cloud. God's presence was an active presence. The LORD was the LORD of hosts, the LORD of armies. He "looked down from the pillar of fire and cloud at the Egyptian army and threw it into confusion" (Exod 14:24). The cloud and fiery pillar was his heavenly throne come down, present on earth. The prophet Isaiah identified the fiery pillar as the visible manifestation of the Holy Spirit: "He brought them through the sea . . . he set his Holy Spirit among them . . . led them through the depths . . . they were given rest by the Spirit of the LORD" (Isa 63:10–14). In the crossing of the Red Sea, the people of Israel were being led by the Spirit, foreshadowing New Testament believers' experience of being led by the Spirit: "Those who are led by the Spirit of God are sons of God" (Rom 8:14).

God commanded Moses and the people to assemble in his presence at Mount Sinai where he spoke to them from heaven in a terrifying, audible voice (Exod 20:22). God promised that when the people later assembled to worship at the place he would choose, "I will come to you and bless you" (Exod 20:24). God would be the main actor in worship, not only receiving praise from the people, but also being there to bless his people. After the covenant was ratified, Moses, Aaron, Nadab, Abihu, and seventy elders were called

63

to the top of the mountain. There they saw the God of Israel and ate and drank in his presence (Exod 24:10). They had a conscious awareness of God's presence that foreshadowed Christ's presence at table fellowship in the early church (Rev 3:20).

God commanded Moses to make a sanctuary—a tabernacle where he would live in their midst (Exod 25:8). God met face to face with Moses and spoke to him and to the people (Exod 25:22; 29:43, 45, 46). Moses was aware that God was speaking to him. He was not just thinking about God; he was interacting with the living God.

God intended that his living presence would distinguish the Israelites from all the other peoples of the earth (Exod 33:16). In the new covenant, God still intends his people to have a conscious awareness of his presence, marking them as a special people, distinct from the surrounding culture. Losing awareness of God's presence diminishes the distinctive biblical character of Christian worship today.

When the wilderness tabernacle was dedicated, God's glory filled it (Exod 40:34). The divine glory, manifested as fire by night and cloud by day, led the people during the years of their wilderness wanderings, again foreshadowing the new covenant experience of being led by the Spirit.

At the dedication of Solomon's temple, the divine glory cloud filled the sanctuary in such a powerful way that the priests could not continue their service (1 Kgs 8:10, 11). Solomon, the priests, and the people had a conscious awareness that God was present. After centuries of persistent disobedience and idolatry, Ezekiel saw the glory departing from the temple, signifying God's absence from the people (Ezek 10:18).

The later prophets prophesied that the time would come when the LORD would bring his people back to the land from exile, and that he would again dwell in their midst (Ezek 34:30; 39:29; Joel 2:28–32; Zech 2:5, 10; 8:3; Isa 4:5; 43:5; 44:3; Zeph 3:17; Hag 2:7). The people would consciously be aware that these promises were being fulfilled.

In the new covenant these promises that God would be present to his people were fulfilled in the ministry of Jesus and at Pentecost. At Jesus' baptism the heavens were torn open (Mark 1:10). Jesus, the beloved Son, was consciously aware that the Father was giving him the Holy Spirit. He knew that he heard the Father's voice. John the Baptist saw the Spirit come down on Jesus in the form of a dove (John 1:32). The centuries-long period of prophetic silence and absence of the presence of the Spirit was over. Jesus was led by the Spirit, tested in the wilderness, and returned to Galilee in the power of the Spirit (Luke 4:1, 14). His entire public ministry of teaching, preaching, healing, and casting out demons was done in the power of the Spirit (Acts 10:38). He manifested the presence of God and God's kingdom (Mark 1:15; 3:14, 15; Luke 10:1, 9). Throughout his ministry Jesus practiced God's presence, looking to God before he acted and listening to God before he spoke (John 5:19; 8:28). Before going to the cross Jesus promised the disciples that he would send the Holy Spirit to be with them forever (John 14:16). They would have a conscious realization of the Spirit's presence, and a new understanding that they were in Jesus and he in them (John 14:20).

---

2. The Felt Presence of the Spirit in Worship

The Negro spiritual "Sweet, Sweet Spirit" expresses the sense of happiness and joy that the presence of the Holy Spirit can produce:

> There's a sweet, sweet Spirit in this place,
> And I know that it's the Spirit of the Lord;
> There are sweet expressions on each face,
> And I know that it's the presence of the Lord.
>
> Sweet Holy Spirit, Sweet heavenly Dove,
> Stay right here with us, filling us with Your love.
> And for these blessings we lift our hearts in praise;
> Without a doubt we'll know that we have been revived,
> When we shall leave this place.[66]

Sensing the presence of the Holy Spirit can make texts like Romans 5:5, "God's love has been poured into our hearts through the Holy Spirit who has been given to us," seem real and personal and enrich our worship with feelings of gratitude and praise.

The Jerusalem church had a conscious awareness of being filled with the Spirit on the day of Pentecost (Acts 2:4). God intended the filling with the Spirit to be a continuing experience in the Christian's life (Eph 5:18). The churches in Galatia knew what it meant to begin their Christian lives in the Spirit and were warned not to continue in merely human effort (Gal 3:2–3). The power of Jesus could be sensed when the Corinthians assembled together, invoking the name of Jesus: "When you are assembled in the name of our Lord Jesus and . . . the power of our Lord Jesus is present . . ." (1 Cor 5:4).

An unbeliever, stumbling into their meetings, might exclaim, "God is surely among you!" (1 Cor 14:25). That unbeliever had some sort of visceral experience that this meeting was different. The early believers knew by experience both Jesus' promise to be present when two or three gathered in his name and his promise to be with them until the end of the age (Matt 18:20; 28:20).

Ralph P. Martin has written that the distinctive mark of early Christian worship was a vivid sense of "the presence of the living Lord in the midst of his own. . . . All the components of divine service were calculated to lead worshippers to an awareness of His presence." This characteristic set Christian worship apart from the other religions of the time. New Testament worship, according to Martin, stood within the "magnetic field of the Holy Spirit."[67]

3. How Awareness of the Divine Presence Faded

For a variety of reasons this vivid awareness of Christ's presence began to fade in the fourth and later centuries of the Christian church. At least eight factors contributed to this fading awareness: 1) the growing practice of infant baptism; 2) the changing nature of

catechesis and preparation for church membership; 3) cessationist beliefs about the gifts of the Holy Spirit; 4) the ritualization of
Christian worship, culminating in the Roman Catholic doctrine of
transubstantiation; 5) the Reformers' emphasis on the sermon as
the central element of the worship service; 6) a faulty theological
understanding of the ascension of Christ and his absence from the
church on earth; 7) a scientific worldview that seemed to exclude
God's direct action in the world; and 8) electronic devices and
social media that absorb Christians' time and imagination. Understanding the effect of these factors can help us recover a vivid and
enjoyable sense of God's presence in worship today.

By AD 600, infant baptism had become the almost universal
practice in Europe. Adult baptisms were becoming rare; except for
Jews, everyone in Europe was assumed to be Christian. Consequently, the promise preached by Peter on the day of Pentecost—
"Repent, be baptized, and you will receive the gift of the Holy
Spirit"—was not experienced as it had been in the context of adult
conversion. The doctrine of baptismal regeneration undergirding
infant baptism held that the infant's original sin was washed away
and that the child had been made a Christian. The newly baptized
infant was unlikely to have had a conscious awareness of receiving
the Spirit. The Holy Spirit, who mediated the presence of the living
God and the risen Christ, was in danger of becoming only an idea
or a doctrine, rather than a felt personal presence.

During this period when infant baptism was becoming predominant, preparation for church membership was also changing.
In the pre-Constantinian church, catechesis was extensive, often
lasting two or three years, focusing on life change and obedience
to the teachings of Jesus.[68] After the fourth century, possibly as a
reaction to the challenge of Arianism and other heresies, the focus
in catechesis shifted from right living to right believing. Right doctrine is, of course, essential for the faith and life of the church. But
the unintended consequence of this change was to shift the focus
of Christian identity from a personal experience of Christ to correct beliefs about Christ. The sense of God's immediate presence in
the midst of the worshipping community was diminished.

A third factor contributing to this change in the nature of corporate worship was the rise of cessationism, the belief that certain spiritual gifts, such as speaking in tongues, prophecy, and miracles, had ceased with the apostles or with the closing of the canon. The historical evidence indicates, however, that these gifts persisted in various parts of the church into the eighth century, though in somewhat attenuated form.[69] Nevertheless, cessationism became the predominant view during the Middle Ages, persisting into the Reformation and modern times. Worship services became dominated by the clergy, and few laity had opportunity to exercise the spiritual gifts mentioned by Paul in 1 Corinthians 12, 14, and Romans 12.

These cessationist beliefs rose in tandem with the growing ritualization of Christian worship, culminating in the doctrine of transubstantiation. This doctrine was given its classic expression by Thomas Aquinas and formally defined by the Roman Catholic Church in 1215 at the Fourth Lateran Council.[70] This doctrine held that at the priest's words of institution, God supernaturally changed the inner substance of the bread and wine into the body and blood of Christ. The outward appearance of the elements remained unchanged. According to this teaching, Christ was in some way present in the physical elements of bread and wine, not in the dynamic and personal way in which the risen Christ was experienced in New Testament gatherings. For example, Christ, through the Spirit, said to the church in Laodicea, "I stand at the door and knock. If anyone hears my voice and opens the door, I will come in and dine with him" (Rev 3:20). The personal pronoun *I* signifies that Christ was personally addressing the people gathered in Laodicea. They sensed that he was doing something to get their attention—spiritually knocking at the door of their awareness to engage them. The scene is one of dynamic movement, with the risen Lord coming to the church in the Spirit to have table fellowship with them. For the Laodiceans, having fellowship with Christ was not merely an experience of receiving a wafer at the communion rail. Rather they sensed that the risen Christ, through the Spirit, was present personally with them, enjoying with them the table fellowship he had enjoyed with his disciples while on earth. The doctrine of transubstantiation, while affirming a real presence of Christ in worship, made this presence less personal, less dynamic, more ritualistic, and more clergy-centered.

The Protestant Reformers rejected the Roman Catholic doctrine of transubstantiation and the teaching that the mass was a meritorious sacrifice for the living and the dead. They did not, however, succeed in coming to agreement on an alternative understanding of how Christ was present during the Lord's Supper. The Lutherans advanced views of consubstantiation; the followers of Zwingli, a notion of memorial presence; Calvinists, various forms of spiritual presence. The unintended consequence was to replace transubstantiation with a sermon as the centerpiece of Sunday worship. This has remained the case in most nonliturgical Protestant churches down to the present.

The sixth and seventh factors, a faulty view of the ascension, and the modern world picture of Newtonian science, are related. Both modern science and common sense seem to teach that the things that are most real are solid material objects we can see with our eyes and touch with our hands. A material object such as a rock cannot be in two places at the same time. Rocks have specific locations. After his resurrection, Jesus had a glorified body but his body was still a physical body. He invited the disciples to see his hands and feet and touch his side. He ate a piece of broiled fish in their presence (Luke 24:39–43). Since we can no longer see or touch Jesus' resurrected and ascended physical body, it may seem that Jesus is absent from the church until he returns physically to earth at his second coming. We hear sermons about a Jesus *who is absent*.

This common-sense view is mistaken. Christ is present with us by his promise and Spirit (Matt 28:20; John 14:18). Jesus' full reality is not just his physical body.[71] It includes his physical body, but it is more. The Logos (John 1:1)—the fullness of the divine nature and the Second Person of the Trinity—dwells in the body of Jesus. "In Christ all the fullness of the Deity lives in bodily form" (Col 2:9). The divine nature of Jesus is centered in his body but is not limited to it. Jesus' divine nature, like the Holy Spirit, is omnipresent, extending throughout space (cf. Ps 139:7–8: "Where can I go from your Spirit? Where can I flee from your presence? If I go up to the heavens, you are there . . ."). Christ is truly present with the gathered church on earth by means of his divine nature and by the Holy Spirit he promised to send to us: "another Counselor to be with you forever . . . I will not leave you as orphans; I will come to you" (John 14:16, 18). The Holy Spirit functions analogously to a "spiritual hologram" who projects the risen Lord into our worship space.

The eighth factor, and a dominant one in today's world, is the pervasive presence of electronic devices and social media. Never has the average person had greater access to images, opinions, videos, texts, emails, information, and entertainment. As any youth worker knows, for the teens in their youth groups, the images on their screens are more interesting than school or church. We spend disproportionate time staring at screens, not fully present to those around us. Digital media shorten attention spans, colonizing imaginations, making it more difficult to focus on the kingdom of God's unseen realities. Minds trained by digital media may find it easier to focus on visible preachers and visible screens than on an invisible Christ who to come to us in the Spirit.

4. Awareness of the Divine Presence: How Can We Get It Back?

To help a congregation recover a more lively awareness of God's presence in worship, the pastor should first pray to God, as did Dwight Moody, for a deeper personal experience of God's presence in his or her own life. On the basis of such personal renewal the pastor can more effectively teach the congregation a deeper biblical theology of worship. The pastor can then proceed to teach some of the biblical passages discussed in chapter one. These texts teach us that worship is not only a human action, but more truly, our human responses to God's actions and presence with us. Even though worship is a regular weekly activity, most churches do not self-consciously examine their theologies and beliefs about worship.

Hebrews 12:22–25 shows that the worship of the earthly church below takes place in the presence of the risen Christ and heavenly church above:

> But you have come to Mount Zion, to the heavenly Jerusalem, the city of the
> living God. You have come to thousands upon thousands of angels in joyful
> assembly, to the church of the firstborn whose names are written in heaven.
> You have come to God, the judge of all men, to the spirits of righteous men
> made perfect, to Jesus the mediator of a new covenant, and to the sprinkled
> blood that speaks a better word than the blood of Abel. See to it that you do
> not refuse him who speaks. If they did not escape when they refused him
> who warned them on earth, how much less will we, if we turn away from
> him who warns us from heaven?

The writer makes it clear that believers gathered below are part of a much bigger picture. The church below is in the presence of the unseen yet very real company above: God, the risen Christ, the angels, and the perfected saints. As the liturgy in the *Book of Common Prayer* declares, "Therefore we praise you, joining our voices with Angels and Archangels and with all the company of heaven, who for ever sing this hymn to proclaim the glory of your Name: Holy, Holy, Holy Lord, God of power and might, heaven and earth are full of your glory. Hosanna in the highest."

The risen Christ himself is the primary agent and leader in true biblical worship; the pastor is the secondary worship leader. God himself calls the people to worship through the human leader's call to worship (Exod 19:10–17). In the sermon, God, by the Spirit, speaks through the human preacher: "If anyone speaks, he should do it as one speaking the very words of God" (1 Pet 4:11).

The congregation should be encouraged to listen not only to the human preacher but rather to listen *through* the preacher to God, speaking through his human servant.

In a true benediction pronounced at the end of a service, God himself speaks through the human minister, imparting grace and blessing the people: "So they [the priests] will put my name on the Israelites, and I [God] will bless them" (Num 6:27). A biblical benediction is not an announcement or a summary of the sermon or a final prayer at the end of the service. In a biblical benediction, God himself imparts a spiritual blessing to his people. The benediction is an act of God, not just an act of a human leader.

Include the concept of the ordinary supernatural when teaching about God's active presence in biblical worship. Teach the congregation that the Holy Spirit is supernaturally present, not only in dramatic ways—signs, wonders, and miracles—but also in the quieter ways such as the opening of the preached word, conviction of sin, true repentance, and forgiveness and healing of longstanding wounds and alienation. Worship "in Spirit and in truth" (John 4:24) is not worship in our natural abilities alone. We need the Spirit to lift us up into the ordinary supernatural, and even, if God wills, into the extraordinary supernatural.

Teach highlights in the history of Christian worship. Many churchgoers are not aware of this history and have ideas and assumptions reflecting only their local church experience. Comment on the ritualization of post-Constantinian worship, the doctrine of transubstantiation, and the Reformation's reaction to the Catholic view of Christ's presence. Note the influence of frontier revivalism's simplified two-part order of worship (praise songs + message) on contemporary evangelical worship.[72] Remind the congregation that in the biblical understanding of worship, the "worship time" (in distinction from the "teaching" time) is not just the time of singing praise songs before hearing a message. Biblical worship includes multiple elements—confession, prayer, hymns, creed, Scripture readings, preaching, offerings, Lord's Supper, benediction—both God's actions and our responses to them.

Consider incorporating more of the parts of worship traditional in earlier church history. These elements could include 1) a specific call to worship and an invocation of God's presence; 2) confession of sin; 3) reading of Scriptures from both the Old and New Testaments; 4) pastoral and corporate prayer; 5) recitation of a creed such as the Apostles' or Nicene; 6) the Lord's Supper; 7) or a benediction, using the words of Scripture. These elements provide more points through which God can touch us between the times of gathering and dismissal.

The teaching on worship can include new analogies from digital technology helping us to imagine how Christ is present with us. The Holy Spirit gives us a high bandwidth, virtual connection with the risen Christ. He is in heaven and we are on earth, but we are connected to him in real time by the Spirit. As noted above, we can imagine that the Holy Spirit brings Christ into our midst as a "spiritual hologram" or avatar. Such images are consistent with texts such as Revelation 3:20, where Christ promised the church that if anyone sensed his presence by faith, he would come and dine with the believer in an active, personal way.

Further elements for worship renewal can include a renewed emphasis on extended times of corporate prayer, and exercise of spiritual gifts as a regular dimension of the services. Before the early church was filled with the Spirit, the believers spent extended times in united prayer (Acts 1:14; 2:4). Every great revival in the history of the church has been prepared for by serious prayer and deeper study of the Scriptures. God did not intend that in the present church age the Spirit would be absent and inactive, but on the contrary, a time when believers would know their spiritual gifts and be encouraged to use them. While it can be awkward for churches with traditional practices to incorporate gifts listed in 1 Corinthians 12, there could at least be a ministry time after the service when people could receive prayer for healing, encouragement, or reconciliation. Such times gives space for God to act outside the confines of our planned orders of worship.

These elements contribute to a recovery of a more vivid awareness of God's real presence in worship. They bring our worship into closer conformity to biblical patterns and can make worship more enjoyable. They also bring fresh energy to our missions and evangelism and strengthen us to stand against the world's secularizing influence.

Practicing God's Presence in Personal Devotion: Meditating on Scripture

Martin Luther, Meditation on Scripture, and Illumination by the Spirit

As an Augustinian monk with a very scrupulous conscience, Martin Luther had no sense of peace with God. He was deeply troubled by the text in Romans 1:17, speaking of the righteousness of God. At that time he understood the term to mean the righteous character of God by which an angry God punished sinners—such as himself. Luther described the spiritual breakthrough in which the Holy Spirit, in the ordinary supernatural work of illumination of Scripture, gave him an entirely new understanding of the text:

> Night and day I meditated on those words. Then I began to understand the meaning: the righteousness of God is a passive righteousness by which the merciful God justifies us by faith. . . . All at once I had the feeling of being born again and entering into paradise itself. . . . I extolled the righteousness of God with as much love as the hatred with which I had hated it. Thus that place in Paul [Rom 1:17] was for me the gate to paradise.[73]

Not only had Luther's head knowledge of the righteousness of God been radically changed; his heart knowledge of God's mercy and grace had become a life-changing reality. The ordinary supernatural illumination of Scripture by the Holy Spirit was the fire igniting the Protestant Reformation.

1. Meditation in the Old and New Testaments

Meditating on Scripture is an ancient spiritual practice with deep roots in both the Jewish and Christian traditions. In our rushed and stressful modern world, meditation can relieve stress and promote spiritual growth.

In the Old Testament period, meditating on God's written revelation was commanded not long after the first written revelation, the Law of Moses, was revealed. God commanded Joshua, "Do not let this book of the law depart from your mouth; meditate on it day and night, so that you may be careful to do everything written in it. Then you will be prosperous and successful" (Josh 1:8). Joshua had the daunting task of filling Moses's shoes and leading the people in battle into the promised land. Meditating on the law of God and obeying it were the key to his success.

Meditation involves a receptive attitude and an unhurried reading of Scripture, engaging the whole person: informing the understanding, touching the emotions, and stirring the will to obey. Meditation may involve both silent reading and reading aloud: "a reading half aloud or conversing with oneself."[74] Hearing the text as well as seeing it helps to internalize it. Mediation helps store God's word in both short-term and long-term memories.

The book of Psalms commends meditating on God's law. Happy and blessed is the one who "does not walk in the counsel of the wicked or stand in the way of sinners or sit in the seat of mockers," but whose delight is in the law of the LORD and who meditates on it day and night (Ps 1:2). Constant meditation on God's law is commended to all. Doing this produces a fruitful and prosperous life: "He is like a tree planted by streams of water, which yields it fruit in season and whose leaf does not wither. Whatever he does prospers" (Ps 1:3).

The godly turn their thoughts toward God during the watches of the night (Ps 63:6) and ponder God's works and mighty deeds

(Ps 77:12). In Psalm 119, the psalmist testifies that he has hidden God's word in his heart as a safeguard against sin (119:11), and meditates upon the precepts of the law because he delights in them (Ps 119:16, 24) and loves them (Ps 119:97). Such affirmations show that the psalmist's engagement with the scriptural text is affective, touching the heart, not merely cognitive or notional. The psalmist testifies that meditating on the law of God has given him a sense of living in freedom of conscience, and wisdom and insight for daily living (Ps 119:45, 24, 99).

In the New Testament, the apostle Paul charged Timothy steadfastly to attend to spiritual practices such as the public reading, preaching, and teaching of the Scriptures (1 Tim 4:15). He directed the believers in Colossae to focus their attention on things above, on the exalted Christ and his work of redemption (Col 3:1). They were to let the word of Christ dwell richly in them as they taught and admonished one another (3:16). Paul encouraged the believers in Philippi to focus their thoughts on things true, right, pure, and admirable (Phil 4:8). During long months of imprisonment, the apostle practiced what he commanded, pondering deeply Christ and the Scriptures. The theological richness of these prison epistles—Ephesians, Colossians, Philippians, Philemon—shows the fruit of that meditation.

In the wilderness, Jesus successfully resisted Satan's temptations by quoting Scriptures hidden in his heart through memorization and meditation. Three times he quoted Deuteronomy (Deut 8:3; 6:16; 6:13). Jesus, the second Moses in the wilderness, quoted the first Moses in the wilderness. Similarly, in public debates with the teachers of the law, Jesus readily quoted from memory texts from across the Hebrew canon (John 10:34 = Ps 82:6; Matt 22:44 = Ps 110:1). Jesus could use the Scriptures—the sword of the Spirit—because he had first memorized and meditated upon them.

On Pentecost, the apostle Peter quoted from memory three texts fulfilled in Jesus' resurrection and exaltation: Joel 2:28–32; Ps 16:8–11; and Ps 110:1. Jesus and his disciples had not outsourced their memories to electronic devices but had hidden God's word in their hearts. We should follow their example today.

2. Meditation in Church History

Meditation can be defined as "devout reflection on a chosen theme, with a view to deepening spiritual insight and stimulating the will and affections."[75] The desert fathers of Egypt and Judea typically spent many hours of the day and night praying and meditating on the Scriptures. In the fourth century, St. Pachomius, a founder of Egyptian monasticism, required those entering his monastery to memorize the New Testament and the Psalms.[76] Such feats of memory, in an age before printing presses and the wide availability of books, now seem incredible in our world of digital devices and short attention spans.

In the sixth century AD, Benedict of Nursia, generally considered the father of Western monasticism, made biblical meditation an integral part of the Benedictine way of life. Benedict expected his monks to spend two to three hours every day in the summer and up to five hours every day in the winter in scriptural meditation and spiritual reading,[77] not staring at their screens—but staring at the Scriptures!

The twelfth-century Carthusian monk Guigo II gave classic expression to what became known as *lectio divina* ("divine reading"), with its four elements of *lectio, meditatio, oratio,* and *contemplatio. Lectio* is the slow, repeated, and reflective reading of the text. *Meditatio* is the leisurely pondering of the words and meaning of the text. *Oratio* is the prayerful engagement with the text and with God in spiritual conversation. *Contemplatio* is the peaceful resting of the soul in God whose presence has been sensed.[78]

Meditating on and memorizing Scripture changed Martin Luther's world and so changed ours. His revolutionary insight into the meaning of the righteousness of God (Rom 1:17) was rooted in his practice of biblical meditation. Luther later reflected on the importance of scriptural meditation in this pivotal moment: "I meditated on those words day and night until at last, by the mercy of God, I paid attention to their context . . . Immediately the whole of Scripture shone in a different light. I ran through the Scriptures from memory and gathered together other terms that also had analogous meanings."[79]

Ignatius of Loyola, the founder of the Jesuit order, made biblical meditation an integral part of his *Spiritual Exercises*, a book which became widely influential in many Roman Catholic and Protestant circles.

In the Protestant tradition, Calvin and the Puritans advocated the practice of meditating on the texts and themes of Scripture.[80] Dietrich Bonhoeffer made biblical meditation a regular part of the daily discipline that he developed for the students in his underground seminary in Finkenwald, Germany.[81] Church history shows that meditation, far from being limited to the Roman Catholic tradition, is a practice rooted in the Scriptures and the practices of the broader church.

3. Meditating on Scripture: Barriers and Benefits

Our world places many barriers between us and the benefits of a slower, meditative reading of Scripture. Too often we feel rushed, distracted, and fragmented. Our phones can deliver texts, products, and entertainment—but also interrupt our conversations and divert us from spiritual things. We need to be mindful when using our devices, in order to remain connected with God through the Scriptures, prayer, and meditation. If reading Scripture on a device, try to avoid the distraction of checking email, Facebook, or the latest news.

The benefits of meditating on Scripture are many. Not only can meditation have natural benefits, such as stress reduction and improved concentration, but more importantly, it can bring us into a deeper experience of the spiritual truths revealed in the Scriptures.

Taking time to meditate and to memorize key texts moves our Bible reading from a merely cognitive to a more holistic experience.[82] We internalize the words, moving them from the outer to the inner spaces of our hearts: "I have hidden your word in my heart" (Ps 119:11). The biblical text can come alive in our present moment with God as he speaks to us through his words, illuminated by the Holy Spirit: "Today, if you hear his voice, do not harden your hearts" (Heb 3:7–8). The word of God is living and active, sharper than any two-edged sword. The Holy Spirit can move the words from our short-term memory to our long-term memory where it can remain to shape our identity and behavior. Some may find it easier to memorize Scripture set to music.

Meditating on Scripture moves our Bible study from our minds to our emotions and imaginations. Meditation can warm our hearts and stir our wills to obey. This ancient spiritual practice can draw us to the goal for which Christ redeemed us, Christ dwelling in us and his character formed in us: "until Christ is formed in you" (Gal 4:19). Meditating on Scripture can be a way to embody the truth of Scripture in our words, deeds, and character.[83]

4. A Biblical Theology for Biblical Meditation

While *lectio divina* is not a new spiritual practice, our practice of it can be enhanced by new reflections on the biblical truths of union with Christ, realized eschatology, and the Trinity. As we prayerfully and unhurriedly engage with the text, we do so as those who are united with Christ, connected to him by the Holy Spirit. We are one in spirit with him (1 Cor 6:17). We are living branches in the true vine (John 15:5). We are living members of the spiritual body of which he is the living head (Eph 4:15). We are the beloved bride of Christ (Eph 5:25, 27). We are friends of the one who opened the Scriptures to his disciples on the road to Emmaus, making their hearts burn within (Luke 24:27, 32).

Because of our union with Christ, our reading of Scripture is a highly personal experience. We have been called to be friends with the one who is the central focus of all Scripture (John 15:15; 5:39.) Christ promised to come and make his home with us and to be present with us until the end of time (John 14:23; Matt 28:20). When we read Scripture prayerfully, in faith, we are not reading it alone, but in the presence of Christ, just as he promised.

We read the biblical texts not only in the presence of Christ, but also in the presence of the Spirit. Realized eschatology means that the age of the Spirit has come. We are those who can now experience the powers of the coming age, which arrived with the resurrection of Jesus and Pentecost. The Holy Spirit came to be an abiding and not temporary presence in the church—to make God's voice from the past a living word in the present. "Today, if you hear his voice, do not harden your hearts" (Heb 4:7).

Augustine: Conversion, Conviction of Sin, Illumination of the Scriptures

In the *Confessions,* Augustine relates his conversion. At a time in his life when he was struggling with guilt and sexual temptations, Augustine visited his friend Alypius in Milan. While in the backyard of an estate he heard a young child's sing-song voice, saying *tolle, lege; tolle, lege*: "take up and read." He believed God was telling him to take up and read the Scriptures. Asking Alypius for a copy of the Scriptures, he opened the text at random, and his finger pointed to Romans 13:13: "Let us behave decently, as in the daytime, not in sexual immorality and debauchery . . ." The Holy Spirit illuminated these words and convicted Augustine of his sin. In that moment, he was converted. When he told his mother Monica what had happened, she rejoiced in the conversion of the son for whom she had been praying for years. Augustine became one of the most influential teachers in the history of the Christian church—and it all started with the ordinary supernatural work of the Holy Spirit, illuminating the reading of a biblical text.

We meditate on the biblical text as those who are privileged to enter into conscious fellowship with the Trinity. Jesus continues to reveal himself to us and to deepen our relationship with the Father. "I have made you known to them, and I will continue to

80

make you known in order that the love you have for me may be in them and that I myself may be in them" (John 17:26). Jesus wants us to experience more of the love that he receives from the Father. Christ and the Spirit work together to enlighten the eyes of our hearts so that we know the Father better—and ourselves better as God's beloved sons and daughters (Eph 1:18; Gal 4:4–6). True biblical meditation brings us into the presence of the triune God: to the Father, through the Son, in the Spirit, so that the love that the Father has for Jesus may be in us and that Christ himself may dwell in us.

5. Biblical Meditation: Practical Steps[84]

While various methods of biblical meditation have been used over the centuries, the following steps can be easily used and adapted. First, choose a quiet time and place. Take a calming breath. Pause briefly, calling to mind what you are intending to do: spending quality time with God in the word. In spiritual direction, this brief pause at the beginning is called *forming an intention* or *collecting oneself*—being intentional, mindful, and fully present in the moment, rather than being robotic, distracted, or divided in attention. Having done this, ask the Lord and the Holy Spirit to illuminate the passage you have selected.

Second, read the passage several times, slowly. Reading aloud can engage other parts of our minds not engaged by reading silently. Engaging our other senses stimulates other areas of the brain.

Third, ponder each word and verse. Try to understand things that may not seem clear. Take time to see connections that the passage may have with other words, images, or stories in Scripture. For example, if our text is John 15, the vine and branches, we may think of the "Song of the Vineyard" passage in Isaiah 5, or the tree planted by streams of living water, bearing fruit in its season (Ps 1). Such connections give us a richer and more textured understanding of the passage. They help us to remember as one text is linked in our memory to others.

81

Take time to listen to God through the text, being alert to how the Holy Spirit may be prompting you to some specific action. In meditating on John 15, the Father's pruning the branches may prompt us to deal with a sinful habit or attitude hindering God's work in us. The Spirit could whisper "Stop visiting those websites" or "Just let it go."

Those who have practiced biblical meditation for many years still find that their minds wander. Wandering is the default condition of our minds. When it happens, gently redirect your attention back to the text. Do not waste mental and emotional energy in scolding or berating yourself.

Fourth, pray back the passage to God. Give thanks for any insights or touches of God's presence you have received. Ask God to help you remember what you have been shown and to live more obediently as a result. If you keep a journal, jot down your insights. That evening or the next day, take a little time to remember your time of meditation. Intentional recollection reinforces the spiritual insights you received earlier in the day.

Whole-brain meditation is an enhanced form of *lectio divina*. This method pairs a narrative text with an expository text so that both visual and verbal processing areas of the brain are stimulated. An example is pairing the scene of the baptism of Jesus with Galatians 4:4–6: "But when the time had fully come, God sent his Son, born of a woman, born under the law, to redeem those under the law, that we might receive the full rights of sons. Because you are sons, God sent the Spirit of his Son into our hearts, the Spirit who calls out, '*Abba*, Father.'" As you ponder this latter text on your status as an adopted son or daughter—having the Holy Spirit—you realize that the baptism of Jesus is a picture of your adoption and reception of the Spirit. In Jesus, by the Spirit, you can see yourself standing with Jesus in the River Jordan, hearing the Father say, "You are my beloved son/daughter; with you I am well pleased."

As you see yourself standing with Jesus at his baptism, turn this truth into a personalized blessing by speaking to God the following confession: "I thank you, my dear heavenly Father, that I am your beloved son/daughter; with me you are well pleased!"[85]

Repeating this biblical truth three times, reinforced with visual images and emotion, imprints this wonderful truth on our hearts.

Practicing God's Presence in Ministry

Ministry in Partnership with Jesus

One late May morning Bob was walking the wooded path around Gordon College's Coy Pond. Going the other way on the path was Cynthia, whom he recognized from church. Cynthia's daughter Ruth had just had surgery for bone cancer, with a long and painful recovery facing her. Cynthia was troubled and weighed down by her daughter's situation, with her two children to care for, and having to reorganize her life for the next months to be care-giver for her daughter. The Spirit prompted Bob, "Can I pray for you and Ruth?" Cynthia nodded, Bob prayed, and Cynthia was grateful for the prayer and concern for her and her daughter.

This was a divine appointment, when God puts a needy person in our path, an opportunity to be a channel of God's grace and compassion. Perhaps as Bob prayed, he was aware of Jesus' promise to be with us (Matt 28:20)—as an invisible but very real third party in every conversation. We, too, can practice ministry in God's presence and in partnership with God.

In the earlier study of Jesus' healing of the paralytic at the pool of Bethesda in John 5, we saw that Jesus never did ministry alone or independently. He always did God's work in the presence of God and in partnership with God. Jesus first discerned what the Father was doing and then joined the Father in doing it. He spoke as the Father directed: "I do nothing on my own but speak just what the Father has taught me. The one who sent me is with me, he has not left me alone" (John 8:28–29).

Because Jesus listened to God before speaking, and looked to God before acting, he could say at the end of his time on earth, "I have brought you glory on earth by finishing the work you gave me to do" (John 17:4). He did not finish all the work that others—even his own disciples—might have wanted or expected him to do. He focused not on meeting the expectations of his followers, but on meeting the expectations of the Father. If we follow Jesus' example, we are less likely to suffer burnout.

Practicing ministry Jesus' way imitates the Trinitarian pattern of Jesus' ministry. The Son acted in partnership with the Father, anointed with the power of the Spirit. We serve in the presence of the Son, who promised to be with us (Matt 28:20). We serve in the presence of the Father, who is in us and among us (Eph 4:6). We serve in the energy of the Spirit, who is with us forever (John 14:15, 17).

William Carey: Missionary Service in the Ordinary Supernatural

Born August 17, 1761, in a small English village about fifty-five miles northwest of London, William Carey recalled that as a youth he was "addicted to swearing, lying, and unchaste behavior."[86] He spent his time with other young people of similar disposition and behavior, much to his father's chagrin. Carey later heard the preaching of the Rev. Thomas Scott, an evangelical minister of the Church of England, and was awakened to his own personal need for salvation. His faith was solidified by reading a book loaned to him, Robert Hall's *Help to Zion's Travellers*.

Carey was a teacher in the village elementary school. As a result of his study of geography and maps, Carey was troubled, realizing that the gospel was not being preached in so many of these regions. "And these are pagans! pagans!" he would cry out to himself.[87] His interest in geography had also been stimulated by accounts of Captain James Cook's voyages of discovery.

These studies laid the basis for Carey's landmark manifesto of the modern Protestant missionary movement, *An Enquiry into the Obligations of Christians to Use Means for the Conversion of the Heathens* (1792). This small book influenced the course of modern history, catalyzing the taking of the Christian gospel and literacy to the distant lands of Africa, Asia, and Latin America. Hearing a sermon in a village church, reading a loaned Christian book, and studying secular geography books and maps were ordinary and undramatic means used through the ordinary supernatural influence of the Spirit to change William Carey's life—and through him, countless others.

As we practice ministry the way Jesus did—in the consciousness of God's presence and as partners with God—we also need to use the measure of success in ministry that Jesus used. This measure was not primarily quantitative but qualitative—focused on the quality of the character and relationships of his disciples. This measure was revealed in Jesus' high priestly prayer. God's ultimate goal is to have a people for himself in which everyone is mature in Christ and enjoys the united and harmonious relationships that commend the message of Jesus to the world (Col 1:28; John 17:21).

In the light of this metric, a church of 650—or even 6,500—may not be more successful in God's sight than a church of sixty-five if those sixty-five embody the Christlike character that Jesus lived and died to achieve.

Finally, how does this theology of the practice of ministry apply to the preparation and delivery of sermons? First, remembering your dependence on God in all things, pray for the entire process of the preparation, delivery, and reception of the sermon. Pray for the Spirit to illuminate the text as you study. Spend time meditating on the text, pondering the words, ideas, and images. Take note of insights that come to mind. Listen to God before going to commentaries and study aids. Pray for clarity of mind while beginning to organize the main points, illustrations, and applications.

Listen not only to God, but also to the people of the congregation. When visiting them, listen actively, with attentiveness and empathy. This quality of listening is missing in many modern social interactions. We can talk at each other without having a real conversation. We can appear to listen while not really hearing the other person. Try to draw the other person out with follow-up questions ("Tell me more about that . . . Are you saying that . . . ?"), rather than just waiting to interject personal experiences. Visiting people in their homes and workplaces and listening attentively will enrich your sermon preparation and provide illustrations for the message.

Be sure to apply the text to the daily lives of your people, not leaving the text in the ancient world of the biblical writers. A sermon that feeds the sheep gives the listener clear answers to two simple questions: "What?" and "So what?" What: What was the preacher trying to say? So what: Why should I care about this and what should I do as a result? Paint the listeners a picture of what this should look like on Monday morning in their own lives. This is a reasonable expectation of those who listen to you.

Consider recruiting people in your church to pray for your preparation, your preaching, and for the worship service as a whole—for the Spirit to anoint you, your message, and the congregation. Years ago, my wife Robin and I visited Bethlehem Baptist Church in Minneapolis. We were impressed not only by the power of John Piper's preaching but also by the joyous singing. We later learned that each Sunday people gathered downstairs to pray for Piper's message and the service overhead.

Finally, after the sermon or ministry event, pray that the Spirit would cause the word to bear fruit in the lives of the listeners. After the service, God remains present to his word. "A man scatters seed on the ground. Night and day, whether he sleeps or gets up, the seed sprouts and grows, though he does not know how" (Mark 4:26–27).

Questions for Discussion

1. Discuss the claim that God's presence through word, Spirit, and sacrament is the heart of biblical worship. Why is a new mental framework for worship needed to recover the power of New Testament and early Christian worship? What features of our modern culture make it more urgent to recover the experience of God's presence in our Sunday morning worship? What practical steps can a pastor or church leaders take?

2. Describe the role biblical meditation played in Martin Luther's spiritual breakthrough that ignited the Reformation. What role does meditating on and memorizing Scripture play in your spiritual life? How is Christian meditation different from Buddhist and Hindu meditation?

3. Discuss the concept of practicing ministry in the presence of God and in partnership with God. How did Jesus practice ministry this way? The apostle Paul? How is this concept related to the doctrines of the Trinity, union with Christ, and realized eschatology? Have you practiced this concept in your ministry? Can you give any examples?

For Further Reading:

John Jefferson Davis, *Worship and the Reality of God.*

How God's active presence in the church energizes biblical worship.

John Jefferson Davis, *Meditation and Communion with God.*

How meditating on Scripture brings us into God's presence.

John Jefferson Davis, *Practicing Ministry in the Presence of God.*

How Jesus' ministry in God's presence models ministry for us.

APPENDIX

A Vision for Renewal in Post-Christian America

THIS BOOK CASTS A fresh vision for the revitalization of American churches, based on a deeper theology of worship, discipleship, and ministry. Churches can rediscover the spiritual power of the New Testament church. In a post-Christian America, churches can do far more than merely survive; in the power of the Spirit, they can actually thrive.

The Global and National Contexts

The contexts in which Christians today are being called to live out their faith differ from those of earlier generations, whether those of Luther and Calvin, colonial America, or the postwar world in which the United States was the unchallenged leader of the free world. Today powerful forces—global capitalism, science and technology, climate change, cries for racial justice and human rights—are altering the global contexts of the Christian church. The pace of change itself is accelerating.[88]

The globalization of the world economy threatens job security for many workers and sparks acrimonious debate about immigration. It keeps believers immersed in a pervasive culture of consumerism, convenience, advertising, and entertainment. Global climate change has contributed to desertification and famine in sub-Saharan Africa, driving tens of thousands of refugees to Europe and other parts of the world, exacerbating existing social and economic tensions. The relentless advances of technology—information technologies, the internet, artificial intelligence, robotics, biotechnology, smart phones, social media—contribute to economic growth and human connectivity. At the same time, they can disrupt institutions and polarize political life.

Many societies, both in the United States and elsewhere, struggle with fragmentation. Political divisions in Washington and between red states and blue states have increased; trust in major institutions has diminished. The tone of discourse on college campuses, the public square, and social media is often disrespectful and harsh. Egregious instances of police brutality exacerbate the racial divide.

The loss of a common national story unifying the nation is symptomatic of this fragmentation. An older American story in which America was a "city on a hill," a beacon of light and freedom to the world, is now challenged by competing secular stories. David Brooks has identified four such secular stories: first, the libertarian story of free individuals, limited government, and the free market favored by the Republican Party; second, the globalized, high-tech America story favored by Silicon Valley; third, the multicultural, identity-politics story of the Democratic Party; and fourth, the America-First story of Donald Trump and others, told in reaction to the second and third.[89] It is not clear which of these stories will prevail in the future.

Perhaps the most powerful challenge to churches' spiritual vitality can be summed up in the word *secularization*. For centuries forces have combined to shift the dominant worldview from one centered on God, the world to come, and spiritual things, to one centered on humanity, this world, and material goods.[90] The Renaissance turned the attention of artists, poets, and writers from biblical and classical themes to a celebration of the human individual in the present world. The Reformation and the wars of religion in the seventeenth century broke the unity of Western Christendom. These religious wars fed the hostility of Enlightenment philosophers toward organized religion and diminished its influence in the public square.

The scientific revolution initiated by Galileo in the sixteenth century and Newton in the seventeenth century was an epochal worldview shift. The new science captured human imagination with images of a clockwork universe—a mechanical view of reality in which God was no longer directly involved in the world.[91] Scientists, not theologians or churchmen, could now understand and control the natural order through the mathematical laws governing material objects in motion.

The Industrial Revolution that brought steam engines, locomotives, factories, textile mills, the telegraph, the generation and transmission of electrical power, industrial agriculture, and much more, gave mankind power over nature unparalleled in human history. Humanity no longer seemed dependent on God for daily bread. Society could provide for itself not just by the sweat of the brow, but with the power of machines driven by fossil fuels.

The nineteenth century that witnessed the massive cultural reshaping of the Industrial Revolution also saw the birth of worldview-transforming ideologies based on materialistic views of the universe. Darwin, Marx, and Freud introduced key ideas of modern secularism. Darwinian evolution replaced a God-designed natural world with one explained by natural selection. Marxism persuaded many intellectuals that human religious and ethical beliefs were not grounded in a transcendent, heavenly order, but were only justifications of the interests of the dominant social classes. Freud secularized the human soul, seeing man not as made in the image of God, but as driven by the subterranean and largely unconscious forces of repressed sexual desires. Biblical critics in Germany and England who had imbibed such naturalistic presuppositions removed the miraculous and the supernatural from the biblical accounts, denied traditional views of dating and authorship, and undermined the authority of the Scriptures as divine revelation.

Later European intellectuals and atheists, such as Nietzsche, Foucault, and Derrida, saw human values not as being derived from a transcendent God or an unchanging human nature, but as humanly and socially constructed artifacts serving the interests of the powerful.

Notwithstanding its benefits in providing new ways for people to communicate and connect, the Information Revolution following the Scientific and Industrial Revolutions reinforced these secularizing trends. New information technologies and social media are producing explosive growth in the quantity of information, but also are making it more difficult for people of faith to focus on spiritual things.[92] An endless stream of entertaining images is constantly only a tap away on the screen. With Amazon, the delivery of almost any consumer item is only a click away. The apostle Paul counseled early Christians to set their eyes on the unseen and the eternal, but screens counsel us to set our eyes on the seen and the temporal (2 Cor 4:18).

Church Life in Today's America

In a comprehensive study of religious trends in America, Princeton's Mark Chaves concluded that "every indicator of traditional religiosity"—whether church attendance, membership, or involvement in religious activities and practices—"is either stable or declining."[93] Belief in the Bible as inerrant has declined, and there has been a trend among practicing Christians away from seeing Christianity as uniquely true.

Membership in the Protestant mainline denominations continues its decades-long decline. What Chaves has described as a "hollowing out of religious beliefs and practices" and an increase in generic forms of spirituality could point to a future, he believes, in which American religion may be less grounded in institutions.[94]

Another striking trend in recent decades is the growth of the *nones*, those Americans who claim no religious affiliation or church membership. Young adults aged eighteen to twenty-nine are three times as likely as seniors to claim no religious affiliation (34 percent vs. 11 percent).[95] Also noteworthy is the steady decline in the percentage of people who report growing up in households with religiously active fathers: from close to 70 percent for those born before 1900 to about 45 percent for those born after 1970. Each new demographic cohort appears to be less active in attending religious services than did earlier cohorts at the same age.[96]

The United States has become a much more religiously diverse nation, with the Christian majority now sharing the religious marketplace with increasing numbers of Muslims, Buddhists, Hindus, and other non-Christian faiths.[97] America's growing religious diversity reflects global demographic and religious changes. The majority of the world's Christians are now the nonwhite and non-European Christians of the global South, in Africa, Latin America, and Asia. In 1910, the statistical center of Christianity was near Madrid, Spain. It is now somewhere south of Timbuktu in Mali.[98]

Globally, Islam now appears to be the world's fastest-growing religion, because of its higher birthrates. By 2060, Islam could surpass Christianity as the world's largest faith.[99] Radicalized Muslims, both in the United States and in other parts of the world, have committed terrorist acts. Persecution of Christians around the world has increased; approximately one in twelve Christians has experienced persecution for their faith. Islamic extremism has fueled this persecution in fourteen of the top twenty persecuting countries, and in thirty-five of the top fifty.[100]

During the 1970s, conservative churches grew in comparison to mainline denominations. In recent decades, however, such trends have halted or reversed, with many evangelical churches experiencing plateaued or declining rates of growth. In the first decade of the twenty-first century, the Southern Baptist Convention, the largest evangelical denomination in the United States, reported membership declines for eight years in a row.[101] In 1988, white evangelical Protestants comprised 22 percent of the American population; now this share has declined to 18 percent.[102] The white evangelical segment is an aging demographic group, and areas of evangelical growth appear to be concentrated in Hispanic, African-American, and Asian churches.

Various observers have argued that postwar evangelicalism became too accommodated to the consumerist and therapeutic

93

values of American culture.[103] During the era of the culture wars, evangelical Christians were thought by many Americans to be too closely tied to the conservative social agenda of the Republican party. Survey data reported by Kinnaman and Lyons found that 55 percent of adult Americans felt that it would be difficult to have a conversation with an evangelical Christian. Even more surprisingly, 60 percent stated that they believed that evangelism—one of the core practices of the tradition—could be seen as a form of extremist behavior.[104]

Previous surveys had shown that many Americans perceived conservative Christians as being judgmental and too political.[105] These impressions were not diminished by reports in the media that in the 2016 presidential election 81 percent of evangelicals had voted for Donald Trump. However, closer scrutiny of these numbers revealed that many of this supposed 81 percent of evangelicals were only nominally identified with the label, and were not regular attenders of evangelical churches.[106] In any case, evangelicals in a post-Christendom America would do well to turn away from top-down politics and identification with any one political party. Focusing on serving neighbors and local communities rather than politics would be a better mission strategy.

Where Have We Come From? Evangelicalism 1.0: Reformation and Revivalism

Evangelicalism 1.0 is characterized by the historical trajectory from the Reformation through the Great Awakening and frontier revivals, to the Scopes trial of 1925. *Sola gratia, sola fide, sola scriptura*—by grace alone, by faith alone, and by Scripture alone, the mottoes of the Reformation—have continued to be central to evangelicalism's identity.[107] Luther, Calvin, Zwingli, and the English Reformers fought to recover the gospel of grace and the primacy of Scripture in the life of the church. Justification by grace alone through faith in Christ alone was the doctrinal center of the Reformation. This doctrine restored the believer's sense of immediate access to God and assurance of salvation. The Bible was

94

made available to the people in their own languages and liturgies. Luther's rediscovery of the Pauline understanding of grace unleashed new spiritual energy and led to a rebirth of hymnody and congregational singing.

The radical wing of the Reformation represented by the Anabaptists made enduring contributions to evangelicalism's later development. Over the course of time, Anabaptist distinctives such as the church as a voluntary association, believers-only baptism, and strict separation of church and state become broadly accepted within evangelicalism.

The Great Awakening of the 1740s, first in the England of John and Charles Wesley and George Whitefield, and then in the colonial America of Jonathan Edwards, left an enduring mark on American evangelicalism. The biblical preaching of Wesley, Whitefield, and Edwards awakened thousands of new believers to the truth of the gospel and brought many into the churches. During a second series of awakenings, beginning at the end of the eighteenth century and extending into the frontier revivals of the 1830s, the doctrine of regeneration—"You must be born again"—became a central emphasis in evangelical preaching and worship.

The fiery evangelist Charles Finney introduced "new measures" for preaching revivals: direct personal address, towns organized in advance of the revival meeting, preaching services on weekday evenings, the call for immediate decisions for Christ. These have remained as characteristic features of the American revivalism down to the present.[108] Finney, Dwight L. Moody, and their modern successors, such as Billy Sunday and Billy Graham, carried the methods and message of frontier revivals to the great urban centers of America, England, and the nations beyond. In this period, evangelicals engaged not only in evangelism, but also in social reform—abolition, temperance, and women's suffrage.[109]

The nineteenth century saw the rise and flowering of Protestant missions, with Adoniram Judson, Hudson Taylor, David Livingstone, and many others carrying the gospel to hitherto unreached fields in Africa, Latin America, Asia, and the Pacific.

The Civil War was a traumatic crisis for the nation, not only politically and militarily—with the death of some 600,000 soldiers from the North and South—but religiously as well. Denominations divided over the issue of slavery,[110] and black and white Christians went their separate ways, worshipping in separate churches throughout the eras of Reconstruction and Jim Crow. The African-American churches, while sharing much of the essential evangelical theology of their white counterparts, maintained their separate and distinctive ecclesiastical identities. They have functioned down to the present day as vital centers for African-American cultural identity, social life, and leadership development.[111]

The post-Civil War period was marked by the bitter and divisive modernist-fundamentalist controversies. The teachings of modernist biblical scholars in Germany and England were brought into American seminaries and churches. Protestant denominations became sharply divided over biblical inspiration and authority. Liberal scholars denied or reinterpreted historic doctrines such as the Trinity, bodily resurrection, virgin birth, penal substitutionary atonement, and the deity and return of Christ. Historic theological schools such as Princeton Seminary, Harvard Divinity School, Yale Divinity School, and Andover Theological Seminary adopted the modernist teachings.

The 1906 Azusa Street revival in Los Angeles marked the birth of modern Pentecostalism. The black preacher William J. Seymour led a revival in which speaking in tongues was seen as the "initial physical evidence" of receiving the baptism of the Holy Spirit described in the book of Acts.[112] The new teaching on speaking in tongues was accepted by some of the earlier holiness churches out of which Pentecostalism arose,[113] but was rejected by others. In later decades, Pentecostalism was gradually accepted and recognized within the broader evangelical movement.

The 1925 Scopes trial in Dayton, Tennessee, pitting Clarence Darrow against William Jennings Bryan, focused on the teaching of evolution in the public schools. The trial was widely viewed as a stinging defeat for conservative Christians and literal understandings of the Bible.[114] By the 1930s, the liberals had largely captured control of the major Protestant denominations. Many conservatives separated from their older, more liberal denominations and founded their own denominations, Bible schools, seminaries, publishing houses, parachurch organizations, and mission societies.

Evangelicalism 2.0: from Ockenga, Graham, and Henry to *Obergefell*

In a 1957 statement to the press, Harold John Ockenga, then pastor of Boston's Park Street Church—and future president of Gordon-Conwell Theological Seminary and Fuller Theological Seminary—declared that "Fundamentalism . . . abdicated leadership and responsibility in the societal realm."[1] Ten years earlier, in 1947, Ockenga had coined the term *New Evangelicalism*, a renewal movement within conservative Protestantism for which he became a leading architect and spokesman. In the postwar period the United States had emerged as the world's leading power, with new energy and optimism. This new optimism was reflected in the movement here referred to as Evangelicalism 2.0.

Ockenga's vision for the New Evangelicalism, shared by Carl F. H. Henry and Billy Graham, broke with the separatist and anti-intellectual tendencies of earlier fundamentalism. While retaining its longstanding commitments to biblical inspiration and historic Christian doctrines, this rebranded evangelicalism aspired to be more socially engaged and intellectually respected in the academy.

In 1947, Carl Henry published *The Uneasy Conscience of Modern Fundamentalism*. Henry called conservatives to combine a passion for social responsibility with fidelity to the Bible. This combination had characterized much of evangelical Protestantism in the nineteenth century, but then diminished as conservatives reacted to theological liberalism and the social gospel movement. The year 1947 also saw the founding of Fuller Theological Seminary in Pasadena, California, a school that its founders hoped would embody the new vision.

---

1. Frame, "Modern Evagelicalism Mourns the Loss," 1.

The 1940s saw the emergence of new evangelical biblical and theological scholarship. E. J. Carnell's 1948 book *Introduction to Christian Apologetics* established Carnell as a leading intellectual spokesman for the movement. In 1949, the Evangelical Theological Society was founded as a central forum for conservative biblical scholars and theologians. The society united around a one-point doctrinal statement affirming, "The Bible alone, and the Bible in its entirety, is the Word of God written, and therefore inerrant in the autographs."[115] In 1959, Carnell, later to become the president of Fuller, published *The Case for Orthodox Theology*, defending historic Christian doctrines but also distancing the movement from earlier fundamentalism.

During the 1950s, Billy Graham emerged as the single most visible American evangelical, with a global evangelistic ministry eventually reaching millions. Graham became a confidant of presidents and served for a time as the chairman of the board of Gordon-Conwell, newly formed in 1969 by the merger of the earlier Conwell School of Theology in Philadelphia and Gordon Divinity School in Wenham, Massachusetts. Graham displayed attitudes and practices that were progressive for the times, insisting that his public meetings be open to blacks and whites alike. Graham also tried to build cooperative relations with leaders of the Roman Catholic Church.

The turbulent decades of the 1960s and 1970s were marked by controversy and social conflict: the Vietnam War; civil rights; women's liberation; Supreme Court decisions concerning contraception, abortion, and school prayer; and changing standards of sexual morality.[116] These decades were mixed ones for the evangelical movement. On the one hand, the Church Growth movement, launched by Donald McGavran and the Fuller School of World Mission, with its homogeneous unit principle, catalyzed the growth of many new churches, including megachurches such as Willow Creek and Saddleback Community Church. The pioneering work of Ralph Winter at the US Center for World Mission in Pasadena put the concept *hidden peoples* on the map and opened new horizons for global mission.

On the other hand, many evangelical pastors and leaders sat on the sidelines during much of the civil rights movement, with skeptical or critical attitudes toward the nonviolent protests and tactics of Martin Luther King, Jr., and his followers.[117] Evangelicals were also generally not early adopters of the environmental movement emerging during this period. In 1947, Carl Henry had called evangelicalism toward greater societal engagement. But with respect to two of the most significant social movements of postwar America, many conservative Protestants were not leaders, but spectators or late adopters.

The American bicentennial year 1976 was a high-water mark for the postwar evangelical movement. Jimmy Carter, a professed evangelical who taught an adult Sunday school class in his Southern Baptist church in Plains, Georgia, was elected president of the United States. *Time* magazine proclaimed 1976 as the "Year of the Evangelical." That same year, David A. Hubbard, president of Fuller, was elected president of the Association of Theological Schools in the United States and Canada (ATS). This was a sign that evangelical scholars and seminaries had achieved the academic recognition Ockenga and Henry had hoped for when launching the movement in the 1940s. Nevertheless, signs of trouble for the movement were beginning to be visible.

In the closing decades of the twentieth century, the movement was sailing through increasingly stormy cultural seas. The ministries of high-profile televangelists such as Jimmy Swaggart and Jim and Tammy Faye Bakker were rocked by scandal. Shocking stories of clergy sexual abuse and cover-ups rocked the Roman Catholic Church. These scandals have damaged the moral credibility and levels of trust in both Roman Catholic and Protestant churches.

Sociologists of religion documented the pervasive influence among American youth of a collection of pseudo-Christian beliefs: *therapeutic moral deism*.[118] This attenuated set of spiritual beliefs included the following: 1) There is a God who created and orders the world and watches over people on earth; 2) God wants people to be good, nice, and fair to each other, as taught in the Bible and in other world religions; 3) the central purpose of life is to be happy and to feel good about oneself; 4) God does not need to be directly involved in one's life except when he is needed to resolve a problem or personal crisis; 5) all good people go to heaven when they die.

The authors of this study, Christian Smith and Melinda Denton, concluded that these beliefs had taken over minds in many American churches, replacing a theologically robust and ethically demanding faith with one that is "only tenuously connected to the actual historical Christian tradition."[119] In a later follow-up study, the same authors found that only 40 percent of the young Christians surveyed (ages eighteen to twenty-three) reported that their moral beliefs were grounded in the Bible or in some other specifically religious sensibility.[120] Many Christian millennials were bringing these beliefs and values to Christian colleges and seminaries as the twenty-first century approached.

Meanwhile, the white evangelical segment of the population continued to age. The median age of American white evangelical Protestants rose to fifty-three, while the median age of Americans as a whole was forty-six.[121]

During the decades of the culture wars, conservative Christian groups such as Jerry Falwell's Moral Majority and James Dobson's Focus on the Family battled against abortion and same-sex marriage. Their activism provoked a backlash among those who saw these efforts as a politicization of religion.

In a 1992 landmark decision, *Planned Parenthood vs. Casey*, the Supreme Court reaffirmed abortion as a fundamental constitutional right, solidifying a core element of the sexual revolution of the 1960s. Justice Anthony Kennedy, writing for the court's liberal majority, expressed the now prevailing cultural belief in the unfettered personal freedom of the autonomous individual: "At the heart of liberty is the right to define one's own concept of existence, of meaning, *of the universe*, and of the mystery of human life."[122] This man-centered declaration was an indication that philosophically, the culture wars had already been won—and not by Christian churches. The logic of *Planned Parenthood vs. Casey* continued to play itself out. It was only a matter of time before the court would extend this logic of human self-definition in the 2015 *Obergefell* decision legalizing same-sex marriage.

In a highly publicized media event that same year, Bruce Jenner, 1976 Olympic decathlon gold medalist, decided to become the transgender woman Caitlyn Jenner, a sign that transgenderism was becoming part of the culture's new normal.[123] Both events signaled the ending of Christendom in America. Biblical and Christian values were no longer the default values for American law and morality.

Evangelicalism 3.0:
Globalized, Diversified, Energized

This closing section offers answers for three questions: In relation to Evangelicalism 1.0 and 2.0, what should be retained? What should be left behind? What new elements need to be added? The pioneers of postwar evangelicalism—Harold John Ockenga, Carl Henry, Billy Graham, and more recently, John Stott, J. I. Packer, and Charles Colson—have passed from the scene. It is not yet clear who will emerge as their successors. The American and global scene has changed dramatically; fresh thinking and vision are needed.

What should be retained from the earlier evangelical heritage? Most who still identify with the tradition would agree that the following should be retained as core commitments: the centrality of the gospel; the inspiration and authority of the Bible; the deity of Christ and his virgin birth, substitutionary death, bodily resurrection, and physical return; justification by faith alone and the new birth; historic biblical teachings on human sexuality and marriage;[124] missions; evangelism; social justice; and fulfilling the Great Commission.

What should be left behind? This question would be answered with less unanimity. Here are suggestions, noted briefly:

Renewal of the Mainline Protestant Denominations: This element of Ockenga's original hopes for the new evangelicalism has had only modest and very limited success. In spite of the best efforts of evangelical scholars and theologians to defend historic views of biblical inspiration and Christian doctrine, and in spite of faithful witness by evangelicals within these denominations, the doctrinal erosion and membership declines in these bodies have not, for the most part, been reversed. These mainline bodies are now, numerically, sideline bodies on the American church scene, with aging members and diminishing membership. This is not to say that evangelicals now in those denominations should abandon them, but rather, that hopes for long-term renewal should be realistically modest.

The Moral Majority and Theocratic Politics: Despite the apparently significant role played by evangelicals in the results of the 2016 presidential election, the longer-term effects of a politicized evangelicalism have been negative. Public perceptions of the movement, especially among younger Americans, have turned more negative, making evangelism and other forms of outreach more, rather than less, difficult. Evangelicals need, in this writer's view, to turn away from top-down strategies and reorient themselves toward more bottom-up strategies, serving their local communities in visible acts of ministry, as faithful witnesses from the margins.[125]

Missing in Action from the Civil Rights Movement: As noted earlier, many evangelical pastors and leaders were on the sidelines during the 1960s and 1970s when the civil rights movement was making advances in American society, with the leadership coming from the African-American churches and their mainline Protestant and Roman Catholic supporters. Going forward, the white American evangelical church needs to be wholeheartedly committed to working for racial justice, understanding, and reconciliation.

Young-Earth Creationism and Anti-Science Attitudes: Since the 1961 publication of *The Genesis Flood* by John C. Whitcomb and Henry Morris, the so-called creation science movement has been a visible and even aggressive presence in many conservative churches.[126] "Creation science" has tended to be associated with skeptical and even hostile attitudes among some conservative Christians toward modern science, especially in such areas as evolutionary biology, human origins, and global climate change. Such attitudes have tended to reinforce perceptions by the general public that evangelical and fundamentalist Christians are scientifically uninformed and intellectually deficient. Such negative attitudes toward science and the public perceptions they reinforce create needless hindrances to the reception of the gospel by the unchurched.

What new elements are needed for the renewal of the evangelical movement, for an Evangelicalism 3.0? Here is this writer's short list:

Deep Catechesis and Discipleship: In order to experience renewal, the evangelical movement needs to recover the intensive and extensive practices of catechesis and discipleship of the pre-Constantinian church.[127] As the culture becomes less Christian, and as biblical literacy decreases both in the culture and in many churches, different practices of discipleship are needed.[128] Pastors and church leaders need a new paradigm for discipleship, one focused not only on teaching biblical content, important as this is, but also on Christian living.[129] The goal of discipleship should be training disciples who *obey all that Jesus commanded.* Churches should measure the success of their discipleship programs, not only by how many participated, but by asking, "Are they actually *doing* what Jesus commanded? Going directly to the person who has offended them and seeking reconciliation? Avoiding lust, anger, and gossip? Forgiving enemies?" The measure of success is the measure to which the disciple of Jesus consistently obeys the commands of Jesus.

Increased Interracial Contact and Understanding: A renewed evangelicalism would increase contact and understanding across the racial divides.[130] Many African-American churches and white evangelical churches have similar theologies, but little social or ministry contact. Many white evangelicals voice a desire for greater racial reconciliation, but reconciliation is not easy to achieve. White Christians need to acknowledge their need for a deeper understanding of the black experience in America, slavery, Jim Crow and the "New Jim Crow," and the mass incarceration of black men[131]—by listening with humility as African-American Christians articulate in their own voices the racism and discrimination they have experienced. Only then can white evangelicals be in a position to understand, to seek contact, and to offer apologies—and even reparation—where these are needed. There can be no rush to reconciliation without first listening, learning, and repenting.

Can this be the time for the white evangelical church to fully own the vision of Martin Luther King Jr., in his historic "I Have a Dream" speech of 1963?

> Now is the time to make justice a reality for all God's children. . . . (M)any of our white brothers . . . have come to realize that their destiny is tied up with our destiny. . . . I have a dream that my four little children will one day live in a nation where they will not be judged by the color of their skin but by the content of their character. . . . And if America is to be a great nation this must become true.[132]

King's vision of a racially just society embodying both personal and social righteousness is a biblical vision needed to heal a divided America and to call a culturally accommodated white evangelicalism back to its historic core commitments.

Partnership with the Global Church in Mission: "Mission from everywhere to everywhere" rather than "mission from the West to the rest" is how missiologists now describe a new era in global mission. In the nineteenth and twentieth centuries American and European missionaries took the Christian faith (together with Western civilization and values) to many unreached areas of Asia, Africa, Latin America, and the Pacific islands.[133] Today, as the numerical center of the world Christian movement has shifted to the global South,[134] missionaries from Asia, Africa, and Latin America are taking the gospel to Europe, the Middle East, North America, and elsewhere. While Christians in North America, the UK, and Western Europe still have the greatest financial and educational resources, Christians from the global South seem to be experiencing greater spiritual power and evangelistic zeal. Many evangelicals in the United States are recognizing the need to see themselves not as the dominant leaders in Christian mission, but rather as partners in mission with emerging leaders of the global South.[135]

The Greening of Evangelicalism: Rachel Carson's 1962 book *Silent Spring* ignited the modern environmental movement. Vivid images of the web of life being poisoned by DDT and other toxic chemicals captured the imaginations of many Americans and created a new social movement. Liberal Protestants and secular people were the first to become energized by the new environmental consciousness.[136] Francis Schaeffer, publishing *Pollution and the Death of Man* in 1970, was one of few evangelicals who were early adopters of environmentalism as a theological concern. Other conservatives were suspicious of the liberal theologies and secular outlooks characterizing mainstream founders of the movement. By 1991, however, Calvin DeWitt's *The Environment and the Christian* showed that environmentalism had begun to move into the evangelical mainstream.[137] Going forward, a "Green" Evangelicalism 3.0 would affirm the integral connections between the

Christian doctrines of creation and redemption, and between the theological valuing of the goodness of creation and human responsibility to care for God's creation.

Toward a More Multicolored Evangelicalism: The leadership of Evangelicalism 2.0 was largely in the hands of white British and American men. The leadership of Evangelicalism 3.0 should include more gifted women and people of color: African-American, Hispanic, Asian, African, and Native American.[138] Such a vision of diversity is a biblical value and a missiological imperative. In God's vision for a redeemed community the dividing walls have been broken down between male and female, black and white, and rich and poor (Eph 2:14–16; Gal 3:28). Native American church and tribal leader Richard Twiss, commenting on the Pauline vision of the unity of the body in 1 Corinthians 12:12–26, asked the timely question, "Could it be that at this time in history God desires for the church in America to give greater honor to those parts that lack it today?"[139] Can white evangelical leaders give greater recognition and honor to Native American, Black, Hispanic, and Asian church leaders?

The apostle Paul stated, "the head should not say to the feet, I have no need of you" (1 Cor 12:21). For too long white evangelicals have in effect said to their brothers and sisters of color, "We really don't need you." A healthy body needs every part to be connected, respected, and valued.

Spirit-Empowered Evangelicalism: The early twentieth-century Pentecostal revivals of Azusa Street, Korea, India, Africa, and elsewhere broke the long dry spell of the Spirit with showers of blessing. In the global South, the felt presence of the Spirit is now a driving force of remarkable church growth and vitality.

Looking to the future, evangelicals need a vision for the church and themselves in which all believers can say, "I know I have received the Holy Spirit, I know I have a spiritual gift, and I know I am using my gift to build up the body of Christ." As the surrounding culture becomes less Christian, the church needs to become more Christian. If the Great Commission is to be fulfilled, if the gospel is to advance in the face of spiritual resistance from Muslims, Buddhists, Hindus, atheists, communists, principalities, powers, and Satan—the church must rediscover the power of the Spirit that Christ poured out on the church in the beginning. To that end, let us work and pray!

GLOSSARY OF TECHNICAL TERMS

Anthropology: in theology, the doctrine of man or the human person. We are *Trinitarian-ecclesial* selves; our core identity and purpose is grounded in our relationships to the Father, Son, Holy Spirit, and to the body of Christ, rather than in the secondary characteristics of gender, race, and nationality. As *extended* selves we are located in our physical bodies, but not contained in them. We are able to extend and connect ourselves to God and to others by our thoughts, words, and hands, and by the bonds of the Holy Spirit.

Epistemology: the theory of knowledge—its sources and criteria. *Empiricism* is knowledge by the physical senses and *rationalism* is knowledge by logical reasoning and inference. Additionally, Christians recognize the *intuitive* knowledge of God and spiritual things. Such knowledge comes through God's general revelation in nature and conscience, special revelation in Scripture, and by word and Spirit—a *word-Spirit* epistemology. God is able to place his thoughts and promptings into our minds. These thoughts and impressions are to be tested by Scripture and common sense.

Ontology: the theory of what types of things are real; whether the most fundamental reality is material or spiritual. *Metaphysics* is a synonym for ontology. In Christian ontology, the Trinity is the fundamental and most important reality. All finite spiritual beings, the material world, and all material things in the world were created by the one, self-existent, eternal, infinite, and spiritual God revealed in the Bible. Spirit is more powerful than matter and material forces, and more eternally significant.

Ordinary Supernatural: the quiet, hidden, undramatic action of God working through a human agent to produce lasting spiritual results. Examples of this level of the Spirit's action include illumination of the Scriptures, conviction of sin, repentance, conversion, and the fruit of the Spirit. An example of the illumination of Scripture and ministry done in the ordinary supernatural action of the Spirit is the Spirit's working through Philip to open the meaning of Isaiah 53 to the Ethiopian eunuch (Acts 8:29–35). The *extraordinary supernatural* is the supernatural action of God working through a human agent in dramatic, visible, miraculous ways. Examples of ministry done in the extraordinary supernatural are God's parting the Red Sea through Moses; God's sending fire on Mount Carmel through Elijah; Peter, calling on the name of Jesus, healing the lame man (Acts 3:1–10). The results of the extraordinary supernatural may be temporary rather than lasting. The 5,000 whom Jesus miraculously fed were hungry the next day and were not necessarily more spiritually mature. The *natural* level of action is the action of God in the processes, people, and structures of the natural order—blowing winds, ripening corn, a beating heart—or human action done without conscious dependence upon or recognition of the need for God's supernatural assistance. An example of human action in the natural would be a pastor who prepares and delivers a sermon depending only his human knowledge, effort, and skill, with little or no dependence on prayer and the Holy Spirit. Of these three levels of action—the natural, the ordinary supernatural, and the extraordinary supernatural—the *ordinary supernatural* is the one most important in ministry for producing lasting results. In prayer, we ask God to elevate our human work from the merely natural level into the level of the ordinary supernatural—or even, if God wills, into the level of the extraordinary supernatural.

Perichoresis: in Trinitarian theology, the interpenetration of the persons and intersubjectivity of the Father, Son, and Holy Spirit, as when Jesus says, "I am in the Father and the Father is in me" (John 14:11). God intends that in salvation, the *perichoretic communion* that exists between the Father, Son, and Spirit be experienced by believers. Believers are united by the Spirit in loving relationship with the Trinity and with one another (John 17:21, 24, 26).

Realized Eschatology: the paradox that the kingdom of God is already present but not yet fully realized. The kingdom has already arrived in the incarnation, ministry, death, and resurrection of Jesus, and in the outpouring of the Spirit at Pentecost. The kingdom will only be fully consummated when Christ returns. In the new covenant, however, believers can experience the *already* aspect of the kingdom, because, since Pentecost, God has made the fullness of the Spirit available to the church.

JESUS' COMMANDS IN THE GOSPEL OF MATTHEW

5:7:	Be merciful.
5:8:	Be pure in heart.
5:9:	Be a peacemaker.
5:12:	Rejoice when persecuted for the sake of Christ.
5:16:	Let your light shine so that they may see . . . good works . . . glorify your Father.
5:22:	No unrighteous anger.
5:24:	<u>Be reconciled to your brother.</u>
5:25:	Settle matters quickly with an adversary.
5:28:	Do not look lustfully at a woman.
5:32:	Do not divorce (except for cause of adultery).
5:34:	Do not swear.
5:39:	Turn the other cheek.
5:42:	Give to those who ask of you.
5:44:	<u>Love your enemies</u>; pray for those who persecute you.
6:2:	Give to those in need, but do it privately.
6:6, 7:	Pray without calling attention to yourself, and pray simply.
6:14:	<u>Forgive those who sin against you.</u>
6:16:	Don't call attention to your fasting.
6:19:	Store up treasures in heaven, not on earth.
6:24:	Don't make a "god" out of money.
6:25:	Don't worry about your daily needs.
6:33:	<u>Seek first the kingdom of God</u>, and all the rest will be added to you.

7:1: Do not judge hypocritically.

7:6: Do not give holy things to "dogs."

7:12: Do unto others what you would have them do unto you.

7:15: Watch out for false prophets.

9:38: Ask the Lord to send out workers into the harvest field.

10:8: Heal the sick . . . drive out demons.

10:28: Do not be afraid of those who kill the body, but cannot kill the soul.

16:24: Deny yourself, take up your cross, and follow me.

18:9: If your eye causes you to sin, gouge it out.

18:15–17: If your brother sins against you, go to him privately and tell him his fault.

18:35: Forgive your brother from the heart.

19:14: Let the children come to me, and hinder them not.

19:17: If you would enter life, obey the commandments.

20:26: Whoever wishes to be great must be a servant of all.

22:21: Render unto Caesar that which is Caesar's . . . unto God that which is God's.

22:37: Love the Lord your God with all your heart . . . your neighbor as yourself.

24:42: Keep watch, for you do not know on what day your Lord may come.

25:13: Keep watch, for you do not know the day or the hour.

25:34–36: When I was hungry . . . thirsty . . . stranger . . . sick . . . prison . . . as unto to me.

26:41: Watch . . . pray . . . so that you do not fall into temptation.

REFERENCES

Chapter 1: Three Crucial Texts for Spiritual Renewal: Acts 2, Matthew 28, John 17

1. Kline, *Images of the Spirit.*
2. Man, *Proclamation and Praise.*
3. Eckman, "Identification of Christ with Yahweh," 145–53.
4. Bauckham, *Jesus and the God of Israel.*
5. Davis, *Practicing Ministry in the Presence of God,* 176–97.
6. For possible meanings of this "breaking of bread," see Schnabel, *Acts,* 179.
7. Experiments in social psychology have found that people who experience a sense of the grandeur of nature have a sense of awe that makes the self seem smaller (Bethelmy, "Transcendence and Sublime Experience in Nature," 509).
8. MacMullen, *Christianizing the Roman Empire.*
9. Keener, *Miracles;* Wimber, *Power Evangelism.*
10. Stevens, *Other Six Days.*
11. Kinnaman and Lyons, *Good Faith.*
12. Kreider, *Patient Ferment of the Early Church.*
13. Kreider, *Patient Ferment of the Early Church.*
14. Chaves, *American Religion,* 110.
15. Lipka, "Religious 'Nones.'"
16. Masci, "Q&A: Why Millennials Are Less Religious."
17. For a list of these commands see Appendix: "Jesus' Commands in the Gospel of Matthew."
18. Kreider, *Patient Ferment of the Early Church,* 231.
19. Kreider, *Change of Conversion and the Origin of Christendom,* 40–53, 73–79.
20. Davis, "Teaching Them," 65–80.
21. Lovelace, *Dynamics of Spiritual Life,* 229–37.
22. Froese and Bader, *America's Four Gods,* 26–30.
23. Williamson, *Shorter Catechism,* Q.1: "What is the chief end of man?" A.:

"To glorify God and to enjoy him forever."

24. Fairbairn, *Life in the Trinity.*
25. The Holy Spirit brings an external relationship to Jesus into an internal relationship of shared subjectivity.

Chapter 2: Three Crucial Teachings for Spiritual Renewal: Trinity, Union with Christ, Arrival of the Spirit

26. Davis, *Practicing Ministry in the Presence of God,* 6–38.
27. Davis, "Doctrine of the Trinity."
28. Barth, *Church Dogmatics* I, 1, 8.
29. Sanders, "Trinity," 35–53.
30. Rahner, *Trinity,* 22.
31. Moltmann, *Trinity and the Kingdom*; Boff, *Trinity and Society*; Torrance, *Christian Doctrine of God*; LaCugna, *God for Us*; Zizioulas, *Being as Communion.*
32. McCall, *Which Trinity? Whose Monotheism?*
33. Wainwright, *Trinity in the New Testament.*
34. Coppedge, *God Who Is Triune,* 50–51.
35. Fortman, *Triune God.*
36. Augustine, *On the Trinity,* x.
37. Aquinas, *Summa Theologica,* i, 2–26.
38. The divine persons are not just relations, but are persons in relation.
39. Heron, "Who Proceedeth from the Father and the Son," 149–66.
40. Muller, *Post-Reformation Dogmatics,* v. 4.
41. Schleiermacher, *Christian Faith,* 2:750.
42. McGrath, *Christian Theology,* 243–71.
43. Cary, "On Behalf of Classical Trinitarianism."
44. Ratzinger, "Retrieving the Tradition," 439–54.
45. Barth, *Church Dogmatics* I, 1, 351. Barth's view that the persons of the Trinity are "modes of being" appears to many to tend toward modalism.
46. As in the ordering of Barth in the *Church Dogmatics,* in contrast to that of Aquinas in the *Summa Theologica.*
47. Coppedge, *God Who Is Triune.*
48. Fairbairn, *Life in the Trinity.*
49. *Westminster Shorter Catechism,* Q.1.
50. Torrance, *Worship, Community and the Triune God of Grace.*
51. Davis, *Practicing Ministry in the Presence of God.*
52. The Christian's partnership in ministry with Father, Son, and Spirit reflects the classic patristic formula: *Opera Trinitatis ad extra indivisa sunt:* the works of the Trinity in time are indivisible—done jointly by Father, Son, and Spirit.

53. "Repose of Venerable Seraphim, Wonderworker of Sarov."

54. Davis, *Meditation and Communion with God,* 41–51, 60–62.

55. Lakoff and Johnson, *Philosophy in the Flesh,* 16–59.

56. Davis, *Meditation and Communion with God,* 55–62.

57. Reading the account of the baptism of Jesus in light of a text speaking of our *adoption* as sons and daughters (Gal 4:4–6), we realize that the experience of Jesus is reduplicated in us by the Spirit.

58. These texts in John 5:19 and 8:28–29 give us a clue as to a possible answer to an otherwise puzzling question: Why are there specific references in the Synoptic Gospels (e.g., Mark 2:35) to Jesus' practice of private prayer, whereas in John's Gospel, there are no references to such instances of Jesus praying in private? The implication would seem to be that, as John came to understand, Jesus was *continuously* in the act of prayer, listening to and speaking to the Father. Jesus is portrayed in John as one who literally fulfilled the admonition to "pray without ceasing" (1 Thess 5:17).

59. Willard, *Hearing God.*

60. Stott, *Between Two Worlds,* 263.

61. Davis, *Meditation and Communion with God,* 35–41.

62. Wesley, *Journal of John Wesley,* 475–76.

63. Schleiermacher, *Christian Faith,* 2:450 (emphasis added).

64. Fee, *God's Empowering Presence;* Wagner, *Your Spiritual Gifts.*

Chapter 3: Three Crucial Practices for Spiritual Renewal: Worship, Meditation, Ministry

65. Davis, *Worship and the Reality of God.*

66. Manna Music, Inc.

67. Martin, *Worship in the Early Church,* 130, 131.

68. Kreider, *Patient Ferment of the Early Church.*

69. McDonnell and Montague, *Christian Initiation and Baptism.*

70. Davis, *Worship and the Reality of God,* 113–70.

71. Athanasius, in his treatise *On the Incarnation,* 3.17, taught the concept of the *logos asarkos*: the body (*sarkos*) of Christ was circumscribed and limited by space, but the Logos (divine person and nature) was not confined to it.

72. White, *Brief History of Christian Worship.*

73. Cited in Isaac, *Prayer, Meditation & Spiritual Trial,* 74–75.

74. Hartley, "Meditation," 305, 306. The Hebrew word *haga* can mean "utter," "mutter," "moan," or even "growl."

75. "Meditation," 882.

76. van Houtryve, *Benedictine Peace,* 135.

77. Tunink, *Vision of Peace,* 268.

78. Magrassi, *Praying the Bible,* 103–19.

79. Isaac, "Monastic Memoria," 130.

80. Calvin, *Institutes* I.2.12.
81. Bonhoeffer, *Meditating on the Word.*
82. Davis, *Practicing Ministry in the Presence of God*, 198–212.
83. As an illustration of "embodied" knowledge, consider how we learn to ride a bicycle as children. We receive verbal instructions from our parents or friends, but we really *know* how to ride a bicycle when cognitive understanding becomes embodied in our new skilled behaviors.
84. Davis, *Meditation and Communion with God*, 122–57.
85. Davis, "Positive Confession."
86. Galli, "William Carey Converts," 11.
87. George, "Faithful Witness of William Carey."
88. Friedman, *Thank You for Being Late.*
89. Brooks, "Four American Narratives," A27.
90. Taylor, *Secular Age.*
91. Dijksterhuis, *Mechanization of the World Picture.*
92. Boers, *Living into Focus.*
93. Chaves, *American Religion*, 37.
94. Chaves, *American Religion*, 113.
95. Jones, *End of White Christian America*, 48.
96. Chaves, *American Religion*, 51.
97. Eck, *New Religious America.*
98. Johnson, *2010Boston*, 6.
99. Lipka and Hackett, "Why Muslims Are the World's Fastest-Growing Religious Group."
100. "Countries Where Christians Face the Most Severe Persecution." http://www.OpenDoorsUSA.org/WWL.
101. Jones, *End of White Christian America*, 55.
102. Jones, *End of White Christian America*, 52.
103. Wells, *No Place for Truth*; Rah, *Next Evangelicalism.*
104. Kinnaman and Lyons, *Good Faith*, 44, 41.
105. Kinnaman and Lyons, *UnChristian.*
106. Beinart, "Breaking Faith."
107. Davis, *Foundations of Evangelical Theology*, 23–34.
108. Rosell, "Charles Grandison Finney."
109. Smith, *Revivalism and Social Reform.*
110. Smith, *In His Image, but . . .*
111. Pinn, *Fortress Introduction to Black Church History.*
112. Hollenweger, *Pentecostalism.*
113. Dayton, *Theological Roots of Pentecostalism.*
114. Larson, *Summer for the Gods.*
115. The Evangelical Theological Society, "ETS Constitution."
116. Lints, *Progressive and Conservative Religious Ideologies.*
117. Heltzel, *Jesus and Justice*; Evans, "White Evangelical Responses to the Civil Rights Movement."
118. Smith and Denton, *Soul Searching*, as cited in Dreher, *Benedict Option,*

10.
119. Dreher, *Benedict Option*, 10.
120. Smith and Denton, *Lost in Transition*, as cited in Dreher, *Benedict Option*, 11.
121. Jones, *End of White Christian America*, 55.
122. Dreher, *Benedict Option*, 44 (emphasis mine).
123. Bissinger, Buzz. "Caitlyn Jenner."
124. Hollinger, *Meaning of Sex*.
125. Hunter, *To Change the World*.
126. Numbers, *Creationists*.
127. Kreider, *Patient Ferment of the Early Church*.
128. Davis, "Teaching Them."
129. Parrett and Kang, *Teaching the Faith*.
130. Emerson and Smith, *Divided by Faith*.
131. Alexander, *New Jim Crow*.
132. King, Jr., "I Have a Dream," paras. 16, 23.
133. Winter and Hawthorne, *Perspectives on the World Christian Movement*, 167–77.
134. Jenkins, *Next Christendom*.
135. Jennings, *God the Real Superpower*.
136. Nash, *Rights of Nature*.
137. Substantial numbers of conservative American Protestants have negative attitudes toward the environmental movement and deny or minimize anthropogenic climate change.
138. Rah, *Next Evangelicalism*.
139. Twiss, *One Church, Many Tribes*, 60.

SELECT BIBLIOGRAPHY

Alexander, Michelle. *The New Jim Crow: Mass Incarceration in the Age of Colorblindness*. New York: New Press, 2012.

Aquinas, Thomas. *Summa Theologica*. 3 vols. Translated by the Fathers of the English Dominican Province. New York: Benziger Bros, 1947–48.

Augustine. *On the Trinity*. In *Nicene and Post-Nicene Fathers*, First Series, vol. 3, edited by Philip Schaff, 1–228. 14 vols. Buffalo, NY: Christian Literature, 1877.

Barth, Karl. *Church Dogmatics I*. Edinburgh: T. & T. Clark, 1968.

Bauckham, Richard. *Jesus and the God of Israel: God Crucified and Other Studies on the New Testament's Christology of Divine Identity*. Grand Rapids: Eerdmans, 2009.

Beinart, Peter. "Breaking Faith: The Culture War over Religious Faith has Faded; in Its Place Is Something Much Worse." *Atlantic Monthly*, April 2017. https://www.theatlantic.com/magazine/archive/2017/04/breaking-faith/517785/2.

Bethelmy, L. C. "Transcendence and Sublime Experience in Nature." *Frontiers in Psychology* 10 (2019) 509.

Bissinger, Buzz. "Caitlyn Jenner: The Full Story." *Vanity Fair*, June 2015. http://www.vanityfair.com/hollywood/2015/06/caitlyn-jenner-bruce-cover-annie-leibovitz.

Boers, Arthur. *Living into Focus: Choosing What Matters in an Age of Distraction*. Grand Rapids: Brazos, 2012.

Boff, Leonardo. *Trinity and Society*. Eugene, OR: Wipf & Stock, 2005.

Bonhoeffer, Dietrich. *Meditating on the Word*. Lanham, MD: Rowman & Littlefield, 2008.

Brooks, David. "The Four American Narratives." *New York Times*, May 26, 2017, A27. https://www.nytimes.com/2017/05/26/opinion/the-four-american-narratives.html.

Cary, Phillip. "On Behalf of Classical Trinitarianism." *Thomist* 56 (1992) 365–405.

Chaves, Mark. *American Religion: Contemporary Trends*. Princeton: Princeton University Press, 2011.

Coppedge, Allan. *The God Who Is Triune*. Downers Grove, IL: IVP Academic, 2007.

Davis, John Jefferson. "Doctrine of the Trinity." Unpublished manuscript, Gordon-Conwell Theological Seminary, S. Hamilton, MA, 2020.

————. *Foundations of Evangelical Theology*. Grand Rapids: Baker, 1984.

————. *Meditation and Communion with God*. Downers Grove, IL: IVP Academic, 2012.

————. "Positive Confession." https://www.youtube.com/watch?v=_xQWUV55tNo.

————. *Practicing Ministry in the Presence of God*. Eugene, OR: Cascade, 2015.

————. "Teaching Them to Observe All that I Have Commanded You: The History of the Interpretation of the Great Commission." *Evangelical Review of Theology* 25 (2001) 65–80.

————. *Worship and the Reality of God: An Evangelical Theology of Real Presence*. Downers Grove, IL: IVP Academic, 2010.

Dayton, Donald W. *Theological Roots of Pentecostalism*. Peabody, MA: Hendrickson, 1987.

Dijksterhuis, E. J. *The Mechanization of the World Picture*. London: Oxford University Press, 1961.

Dreher, Rod. *The Benedict Option: A Strategy of Christians in a Post-Christian Nation*. New York: Random House, 2017.

Eck, Diana L. *A New Religious America: How a "Christian Country" Has Become the World's Most Religiously Diverse Nation*. New York: HarperCollins, 2001.

Eckman, Edward. "The Identification of Christ with Yahweh by New Testament Writers." *Gordon Review* 7:4 (1964) 145–53.

Emerson, Michael O., and Christian Smith. *Divided by Faith: Evangelical Religion and the Problem of Race in America*. New York: Oxford University Press, 2000.

The Evangelical Theological Society. "ETS Constitution." http://www.etsjets.org/about/constitution.

Evans, C. J. "White Evangelical Responses to the Civil Rights Movement." *Harvard Theological Review* 102:2 (2009) 245–73.

Fairbairn, Donald. *Life in the Trinity: An Introduction to Theology with the Help of the Fathers*. Downers Grove, IL: InterVarsity, 2009.

Fee, Gordon D. *God's Empowering Presence: The Holy Spirit in the Letters of Paul*. Peabody, MA: Hendrickson, 1994.

Fortman, Eugene. *The Triune God: A Historical Study of the Doctrine of the Trinity*. Grand Rapids: Baker, 1982.

Frame, Randy. "Modern Evangelicalism Mourns the Loss of One of Its Founding Fathers." *Christianity Today*, March 15, 1985. https://www.christianitytoday.com/ct/1985/march-15/modern-evangelicalism-mourns-loss-of-one-of-its-founding.html.

Friedman, Thomas L. *Thank You For Being Late*. New York: Farrar, Straus and Giroux, 2016.

Froese, Paul, and Christopher Bader. *America's Four Gods What We Say about God and What That Says about Us*. New York: Oxford University Press, 2015.

Galli, Mark. "William Carey Converts." *Christian History* 11:4 (1992) 10–11.

George, Timothy. "The Faithful Witness of William Carey." https://missionexus. org/the-faithful-witness-of-william-carey/.

Graves, Dan. "Article #29." https://christianhistoryinstitute.org/incontext/ article/aquinas.

Gunton, Colin. *The Promise of Trinitarian Theology*. Edinburgh: T. & T. Clark, 1991.

Hartley, J. E. "Meditation." In *International Standard Bible Encyclopedia*, vol. 3, edited by Geoffrey W. Bromiley, 305–6. 4 vols. Grand Rapids: Eerdmans, 1986.

Heltzel, Peter. *Jesus and Justice: Evangelicals, Race, and American Politics*. New Haven: Yale University Press, 2009.

Heron, A. I. C. "Who Proceedeth from the Father and the Son: The Problem of the Filioque." *Scottish Journal of Theology* 24 (1971) 149–66.

Hollenweger, Walter J. *Pentecostalism: Origins and Developments Worldwide*. Peabody, MA: Hendrickson, 2005.

Hollinger, Dennis P. *The Meaning of Sex: Christian Ethics and the Moral Life*. Grand Rapids: Baker Academic, 2009.

Hunter, James Davison. *To Change the World*. New York: Oxford University Press, 2010.

Isaac, Gordon. "Monastic Memoria in the Preface to the Complete Edition of Luther's Latin Writings 1545." *Luther Digest* 20 (2012) 127–40.

———. *Prayer, Meditation & Spiritual Trial: Luther's Account of Life in the Spirit*. Peabody, MA: Hendrickson, 2017.

Jenkins, Philip. *The Next Christendom: The Coming of Global Christianity*. New York: Oxford University Press, 2002.

Jennings, J. Nelson. *God the Real Superpower: Rethinking Our Role in Mission*. Phillipsburg, NJ: Presbyterian & Reformed, 2007.

Johnson, Todd M. et al., eds. *2010Boston: The Changing Contours of World Mission and Christianity*. Eugene, OR: Pickwick, 2012.

Jones, Robert P. *The End of White Christian America*. New York: Simon & Schuster, 2016.

Keener, Craig. *Miracles: The Credibility of the New Testament Claims*. Grand Rapids: Baker 2011.

King, Martin Luther, Jr. "I Have a Dream." https://kinginstitute.stanford.edu/ king-papers/documents/i-have-a-dream-address-delivered-march- washington-jobs-and-freedom.

Kinnaman, David, and Gabe Lyons. *Good Faith: Being a Christian When Society Thinks You Are Irrelevant and Extreme*. Grand Rapids: Baker, 2016.

———. *UnChristian: What a New Generation Really Thinks about Christianity . . . and Why It Matters*. Grand Rapids: Baker, 2007.

Kline, Meredith G. *Images of the Spirit*. Eugene, OR: Wipf & Stock, 1999.

Kreider, Alan. *The Change of Conversion and the Origin of Christendom*. Eugene, OR: Wipf & Stock, 2006.

———. *The Patient Ferment of the Early Church: The Improbable Rise of Christianity in the Roman Empire*. Grand Rapids: Baker Academic, 2016.

Lacugna, Catherine Mowry. *God for Us: The Trinity and the Christian Life*. New York: HarperOne, 2000.

Lakoff, George and Mark Johnson. *Philosophy in the Flesh: The Embodied Mind and Its Challenge to Western Thought*. New York: Basic, 1999.

Larson, Edward J. *Summer for the Gods*. Cambridge, MA: Harvard University Press, 1997.

Lints, Richard. *Progressive and Conservative Religious Ideologies: The Turbulent Decade of the 1960s*. New York: Ashgate, 2010.

Lipka, Michael. "Religious 'Nones' Are Not Only Growing, They're Becoming More Secular." Pew Research Center. https://www.pewresearch.org/fact-tank/2015/11/11/religious-nones-are-not-only-growing-theyre-becoming-more-secular/.

Lipka, Michael, and Conrad Hackett. "Why Muslims Are the World's Fastest-Growing Religious Group." *Pew Research Center*, April 6, 2017. http://www.pewresearch.org/fact-tank/2017/04/06/why-muslims-are-the-worlds-fastest-growing-religious-group/.

Lovelace, Richard. *Dynamics of Spiritual Life: An Evangelical Theology of Renewal*. Downers Grove, IL: InterVarsity, 1979.

MacMullen, Ramsey. *Christianizing the Roman Empire: A.D. 100–400*. New Haven: Yale University Press, 1984.

Magrassi, Mariona. *Praying the Bible: An Introduction to Lectio Divina*. Translated by Edward Hagman. Collegeville, MN: Liturgical, 1968.

Man, Ron. *Proclamation and Praise: Hebrews 2:12 and the Christology of Worship*. Eugene, OR: Wipf & Stock, 2007.

Martin, Ralph P. *Worship in the Early Church*. London: Marshall, Morgan & Scott, 1964.

Masci, David. "Q&A: Why Millennials Are Less Religious." Pew Research Center. www.pewresearch.org/fact-tank/2016/01/08/.

McCall, Thomas. *Which Trinity? Whose Monotheism?* Grand Rapids: Eerdmans, 2010.

McDonnell, Kilian, and George T. Montague. *Christian Initiation and Baptism in the Holy Spirit: Evidence from the First Eight Centuries*. Collegeville, MN: Liturgical, 1991.

McGrath, Alister E. *Christian Theology: An Introduction*. Malden, MA: Wiley, Blackwell, 2017.

"Meditation." In *The Oxford Dictionary of the Christian Church*, edited by F.L. Cross, 882. New York: Oxford University Press, 1974.

Moltmann, Jurgen. *The Trinity and the Kingdom*. Philadelphia: Fortress, 1980.

SELECT BIBLIOGRAPHY

Muller, Richard. *Post-Reformation Dogmatics.* 2nd ed. 4 vols. Grand Rapids: Baker Academic, 2003.

Nash, Roderick Frazier. *The Rights of Nature: A History of Environmental Ethics.* Madison: University of Wisconsin Press, 1989.

Numbers, Ronald L. *The Creationists: The Evolution of Scientific Creationism.* Berkeley: University of California Press, 1992.

Parrett, Gary A. and S. Steve Kang. *Teaching the Faith, Forming the Faithful: A Biblical Vision for Education in the Church.* Downers Grove, IL: IVP Academic, 2009.

Pinn, Anne H., and Anthony B. Pinn. *Fortress Introduction to Black Church History.* Minneapolis: Fortress, 2002.

Rah, Soong-Chan. *The Next Evangelicalism: Freeing the Church from Western Cultural Captivity.* Downers Grove, IL: InterVarsity, 2009.

Rahner, Karl. *The Trinity.* New York: Herder and Herder, 1970.

Ratzinger, Joseph. "Retrieving the Tradition: Concerning the Notion of Person in Theology." *Communio* 17:3 (1990) 439–54.

"Repose of Venerable Seraphim, Wonderworker of Sarov." https://www.oca.org/saints/lives/2000/01/02/100008-repose-of-venerable-seraphim-wonderworker-of-sarov.

Rosell, Garth M. "Charles Grandison Finney and the Rise of the Benevolence Empire." PhD diss., University of Minnesota, 1971.

Ruthven, Jon. *On the Cessation of the Charismata: The Protestant Polemic on Postbiblical Miracles.* Sheffield, UK: Sheffield Academic, 1993.

Sanders, Fred. "The Trinity." In *The Oxford Handbook of Systematic Theology,* edited by John Webster et al., 35–53. New York: Oxford University Press, 2007.

Schnabel, Eckhard J. *Acts.* Grand Rapids: Zondervan, 2012.

Schleiermacher, Friedrich. *The Christian Faith.* English Translation of the Second German Edition. 2 vols. Edited by H. R. Mackintosh and J. S. Stewart. New York: Harper Torchbooks, 1963.

Smith, H. Shelton. *In His Image, but . . . Racism in Southern Religion, 1780–1910.* Durham, NC: Duke University Press, 1972.

Smith, Timothy L. *Revivalism and Social Reform in Mid-Nineteenth-Century America.* Nashville: Abingdon, 1957.

Stevens, R. Paul. *The Other Six Days: Vocation, Work, and Ministry in Biblical Perspective.* Grand Rapids: Eerdmans, 2000.

Stott, John R. W. *Between Two Worlds.* Grand Rapids: Eerdmans, 1982.

Taylor, Charles. *A Secular Age.* Cambridge, MA: Harvard University Press, 2007.

Torrance, James B. *Worship, Community and the Triune God of Grace.* Downers Grove, IL: InterVarsity, 1996.

Torrance, Thomas F. *The Christian Doctrine of God, One Being Three Persons.* Edinburgh: T. & T. Clark, 1996.

Tunink, Wilfrid. *Vision of Peace: A Study of Benedictine Monastic Life.* New York: Farrar, Straus, 1963.

Turkle, Sherry. *Reclaiming Conversation: The Power of Talk in a Digital Age.* New York: Penguin, 2015.

Twiss, Richard. *One Church, Many Tribes: Following Jesus the Way God Made You.* Ventura, CA: Regal, 2000.

van Houtryve, Dom Idesbald. *Benedictine Peace.* Westminster, MD: Newman, 1950.

Wagner, C. Peter *Your Spiritual Gifts Can Help Your Church Grow.* Ventura, CA: Regal, 1979.

Wainwright, Arthur W. *The Trinity in the New Testament.* London: SPCK, 1969.

Wells, David F. *No Place for Truth: Or Whatever Happened to Evangelical Theology?* Grand Rapids: Eerdmans, 1993.

Wesley, John. *The Journal of John Wesley,* vol. 1. 8 vols. Edited by Nehemiah Curnock. London: Charles H. Kelly, n.d.

White, James F. *A Brief History of Christian Worship.* Nashville: Abingdon, 1993.

Willard, Dallas. *Hearing God: Developing a Conversational Relationship with God.* Downers Grove, IL: InterVarsity, 2012.

Williamson, G. I. *The Shorter Catechism.* Nutley, NJ: Presbyterian and Reformed, 1970.

Wimber, John. *Power Evangelism: Signs and Wonders Today.* London: Hodder and Stoughton, 1985.

Winter, Ralph D., and Steven C. Hawthorne, eds. *Perspectives on the World Christian Movement: Reader.* Pasadena, CA: William Carey, 1982.

Zizioulas, John. *Being as Communion.* Crestwood, NY: St. Vladimir's Seminary Press, 1985.

Zuckerman, Phil. *Living the Secular Life.* New York: Penguin, 2014.